THIS OLD GAL'S

PRESSURE COOKER

COOKBOOK

BY JILL SELKOWITZ

Creator of *This Old Gal*

NEARLY 100 EASY AND DELICIOUS RECIPES FOR YOUR INSTANT POT AND PRESSURE COOKER

Race Point
PUBLISHING

Without his teachings, this book would not have been possible. Thank you, Dad.

Brimming with creative inspiration, how-to projects, and useful information to enrich your everyday life, Quarto Knows is a favorite destination for those pursuing their interests and passions. Visit our site and dig deeper with our books into your area of interest: Quarto Creates, Quarto Cooks, Quarto Homes, Quarto Lives, Quarto Drives, Quarto Explores, Quarto Gifts, or Quarto Kids.

Inspiring | Educating | Creating | Entertaining

Text © 2018 by Jill Selkowitz

First published in 2018 by Race Point,
an imprint of The Quarto Group,
142 West 36th Street, 4th Floor,
New York, NY 10018, USA
T (212) 779-4972 **F** (212) 779-6058
www.QuartoKnows.com

Race Point titles are also available at discount for retail, wholesale, promotional, and bulk purchase. For details, contact the Special Sales Manager by email at specialsales@quarto.com or by mail at The Quarto Group, Attn: Special Sales Manager, 401 Second Avenue North, Suite 310, Minneapolis, MN 55401, USA.

10 9 8 7 6 5 4 3 2 1

ISBN: 978-1-63106-488-3

Editorial Director: Jeannine Dillon
Managing and Project Editor: Erin Canning
Photography: Glenn Scott Photography
Cover and Interior Design: Amy Harte 3&Co. and Philip Buchanan

Printed in China

Contents

Introduction

Confession

Cooking and eating are both deeply personal to me. I was passionate in creating this cookbook, not just because of the recipes, but because I hope others will benefit from its usefulness—mainly great meals, but also to bolster fun, confidence, and the joy of knowing that they can make delicious, nourishing food, even with a busy lifestyle.

For me, food is not just about nourishment; it is about the journey from start to finish—from grocery shopping, to prepping, to cooking, to plating. It is all an experience. And for each person, that experience is different. In cooking for others, I feel that I am sharing my story.

I enjoy hosting guests for dinner because it allows me to show them who I am sans words. They can taste the passion and joy of my cooking and know that I had them in mind when making it. While I am not born in confidence, I can attest to my recipes. Have I created a meal and perfected it on the first try? Yes. Have I failed on the first try? Yes. Those failures only pushed me to work harder to create a catalog of recipes that I could feel confident publishing. I have repeatedly tested all of my recipes to make sure that my directions are clear.

In all honesty, that is where I am less confident. How do I communicate the warm earthiness of a sofrito, the excitement of spices, and the comfort of a home-cooked meal using only words? How do you describe a hearty soup without being prosaic? How do I explain a fork-tender pot roast in prose alone? With time ticking, I took a step back, cleared my mind, and waited for inspiration.

It came to me just like the wafting smell of a delicious meal. "I can be my own aroma of roasted garlic and grilled onions," metaphorically speaking, of course. Throughout this book, I share some of my story, in hopes that I can convey to you this important message: You can prepare delicious, nourishing food for yourself, loved ones, and friends. You can incorporate from-scratch cooking into your life, no matter how busy a life you lead. You may even be surprised to discover that it may take less of your time to cook at home than it does to order and pick up a take-out meal. And, eventually, you will notice a savings in time and money.

Who am I, and why did I write a book?

My name is Jill Selkowitz. I enjoy traveling, attending live theater, hanging out with my Tonkinese kitties and my guy, and, of course, cooking and eating. People who have found this book by way of my Facebook group (https://www.facebook.com/groups/ThisOldGal), or my food blog (https://thisoldgal.com), probably know these things about me already. For those who don't know me, here is a little introduction into *This Old Gal*.

I grew up in Miami with my father. He put himself through law school as a short-order cook, so I had a private cooking instructor right in my own kitchen. My dad loved to entertain. I remember growing up with fancy dinner parties equipped with Armetale, crystal wine goblets, good friends, and tasty food. My dad was very social and loved the finer things in life.

Like my dad, I love food and experimenting with all kinds of ingredients and all types of cooking methods. To this day, I appreciate the peace and calm of being in the kitchen, the grace of creating things that sustain and nourish me and sharing that with others.

My dad hired me as his legal secretary so that he could teach me the skills needed to become an excellent legal secretary, as he knew I was planning to move to Los Angeles. That career gave me mobility. In May of 1985, I moved to Los Angeles with my cocker spaniel, Buffy, found an apartment, and took a job as a legal secretary.

That was a great, stable job that still allowed me to do the things I loved because my passion for cooking and feeding my friends continued.

Being in Los Angeles, I decided to pursue acting in my free time. I also began teaching aerobics for Richard Simmons at his studio, Slimmons. I then found myself lucky to be cast as a dancer in Richard's Sweatin' to the Oldies 3 video. While it was a lot of fun, I still found myself wanting something more.

Looking for a change of scenery, and with a car full of kitties, I moved to Charleston, South Carolina, in 2003. Charleston is such a beautiful city with incredible cuisine, history, and culture. This is where I learned a lot about good ol' Southern cooking. After a few years there, I opted to move back to Florida. I always found myself moving to different parts of Florida, from Boynton Beach to Miami. Still, even with my love of Cuban food, I knew deep down, I always felt that Los Angeles was home. So, I followed my heart and moved back. Its air, light, and rhythms just seem to fit me. Something about Los Angeles makes me feel at ease and I know that this is home.

Making food and sharing it with people, while empowering others with the knowledge and skills to do the same for themselves—these are my constants, the anchors in my life. I love learning about local, regional, and international ingredients and recipes. I also love finding ways to make them accessible to people in other regions. The Internet has made it possible to connect with others who enjoy cooking worldwide. My real-world experiences, and interest in all things culinary, are what push me each day to keep doing what I do. Over the years, I have participated in numerous groups, shared many recipes, and answered tons of questions about various cooking methods and techniques.

I began cooking with electric pressure cookers in 2004. By 2011, I was also using multi-cookers, such as the Instant Pot. In recent years, their popularity has skyrocketed among cooks of all interests and levels of experience. I think the time-saving factor is a major reason for this, as well as the safety and sophistication of the technology. These multi-cooker pressure cookers offer many functions and can be used to replace single-task appliances, such as electric pressure cookers, rice cookers, steamers, and slow cookers. Along with this popularity boom, I have experienced an increase in the number of questions I am asked about pressure cooking. I knew that there had to be a way for me to share my knowledge with others more readily. Enter blogging.

About two and a half years ago when I discovered blogging, I decided that this was something that I could do and, as it turned out, it was exactly what I was looking for. I quickly created ThisOldGal.com. I designed it as a place where I could create archives of my personal recipes, create new and exciting ones, and offer tips to help and encourage others. I am incredibly lucky to be doing what I love, fulfilling my passion of cooking, and teaching, while also making a living.

As with the Facebook group, I am the woman behind the curtain, posting recipes and tips, and responding to questions and comments. I am on a campaign to demystify home cooking. I want people to understand that electric pressure cookers can add tremendous value to their already busy lives. It is possible to work, take care of family and friends, run errands, make home repairs, hit the gym, take the kids to practice, and still have time to prepare and enjoy a wonderful meal.

I hope you will enjoy these recipes as much as I enjoyed creating them.

The blog and the This Old Gal online groups continue to be a rich source of support, sharing, and learning together. You are welcome to join in the community and the fun!

https://www.facebook.com/groups/ThisOldGal, and, of course, the blog, https://thisoldgal.com.

Happy Pressure Cooking!

TOG PRESSURE COOKING TIPS

How Is Pressure Created?

Pressure is created by boiling liquid, such as water, chicken broth, or even the water released from vegetables and some types of meat. As the liquid is trapped inside a sealed, air-proof chamber, it won't evaporate as it would when being cooked on the stove or in an oven; therefore, you always want to use the least amount of liquid possible, just enough to cook the food (except for times when you do want the food to boil in liquid, like when cooking a corned beef or making soups and stews.)

Hot Pot, Cold Oil

Adding cold oil to a hot cooking pot helps to make a stainless steel pot nonstick. For any recipe, using the Sauté function before pressure cooking, it is important to fully heat the cooking pot prior to adding the fat (i.e., oil, butter, etc.). Doing this will help when deglazing the pot after sautéing, as the stuck-on browned bits will easily release from the bottom of the pot.

Deglazing the Cooking Pot

Deglazing is a cooking technique, where liquid is used to remove and dissolve browned food residue (called "fond") from the bottom of the cooking pot after sautéing. Liquids may include cooking sauces, wine, beer, stocks, fruit and vegetable juices, etc. Once you pour the liquid into the hot pot, it will begin to simmer and the bits will start to release. Use a spatula to scrape the bottom of the pot until nothing is stuck. This is a very important step that is necessary for the pot to pressurize. If anything is left stuck on the bottom, you may get a burn warning.

Quick Pressure Release and Natural Pressure Release

A Quick Pressure Release is a manual, hands-on method of releasing the pressure from inside the sealed cooking pot. The pressure valve is moved from seal to vent. This act causes the built-up steam/pressure from inside the sealed environment to quickly escape through a small opening in the pressure release valve. When doing a Quick Pressure Release, it is best to toggle the pressure valve back and forth to slowly release the pressure. By toggling the valve, you can control the amount of pressure being released and avoid any food from escaping through the valve and causing a mess. The safest way to release the pressure is with your thumb and first finger (not with a long tool!). Just make sure not to have your hands or body directly over the valve as pressure is being released.

A Natural Pressure Release is when the user does nothing and allows the pressure cooker to slowly release the pressure itself. Remember, "natural" means not caused by humankind. You can walk out of the kitchen and not worry that you need to be standing guard to release pressure when you hear the beep. By allowing the pressure to release naturally, food spewing out of the float valve won't be an issue.

Timing the Recipes

There are three steps, which make up the timing of my recipes:

1. The time it takes for the pot to pressurize.

2. The pressure cooking time, which is the time indicated with each recipe in this book.

3. The time it takes for the pressure to release, whether it be by a Quick Pressure Release or a partial to full Natural Pressure Release.

Most of my recipes have a short cook time and use the Natural Pressure Release time to continue cooking the food at a gentler pace. Using my three-step process for pressure cooking makes a difference in the outcome of the recipes. For example, with the right cooking method, you will never have a dry or rubbery piece of chicken using one of my recipes. If ever a recipe seems undercooked to your tastes, just put the lid back on the pressure cooker and cook it for 5 minutes more. Some things might take longer to cook based on a number of factors and variables.

Safety and Cleaning Tips

Your pressure Cooker should never be used directly on your stove-top burners. It is a fire hazard, as someone might accidentally hit the burner knob and turn on the flame or element. If your kitchen is small and you need the extra space, there are covers for the stove -top burners, which double as a cutting board.

If you are not using your stove, a good idea is to remove the knobs and store them in a drawer.

Make sure all pressure is released before opening the lid. When pressure is reached, the float valve—the little silver cylindrical piece of metal that moves up and down—will be up. It will not retreat down until all the pressure has been released from the pot. Once the float valve has moved back down into the lid, the pressure has been released and the lid is safe to remove.

Always wash the lid of the pressure cooker, in addition to the cooking pot, silicone ring, pressure valve, and float valve. The silicone sealing ring also should be removed and washed. After the lid has dried, store it upside down on top of the base of the pressure cooker. This is great way to air-dry the lid, as you don't want to seal it up with the moisture still inside.

ESSENTIAL TOG TIPS, TOOLS, AND KITCHEN ACCESSORIES

Pasta (General Rule of Thumb)

Check the pasta's packaging for the range of cooking time. Take the shorter time and then subtract 2 minutes (e.g., if the package says that the cook time is 8 to 11 minutes, then use the cook time of 6 minutes on the pressure cooker). Let the pressure cooker naturally release for 5 minutes, and then do a manual, controlled quick release. If you prefer a softer noodle, use the same method, but wait 7 to 10 minutes for a softer result.

Starch Protection Method (SPM)

I use potato starch in many of my recipes, which is a trick I discovered several years ago. My SPM for first dredging chicken in potato starch and then searing it ensures that the chicken is moist, tender, and juicy. The potato starch protects the chicken and locks in the moisture. It is also helpful for other types of meat as it makes sautéing much easier. The food won't stick to the bottom of the pot, and in the case of meatballs (pages 54, 63, 68, and 144) and Salisbury Steak (page 64), it helps keep the meat from breaking apart. Not only does it facilitate the cooking process, but it also acts as a thickener, making a slurry unnecessary.

Cheese

I prefer Asiago over Parmesan cheese for any recipe that calls for either. For all types of cheese, always buy a block of cheese and use a cheese grater or shredder, to shred it yourself. The cheese that comes already shredded has a cornstarch coating, which dries out the cheese.

Mushrooms

For recipes that call for mushrooms, cremini mushrooms work better than the white button mushrooms. Cremini are often referred to as baby bellas, or small portobello mushrooms. The button mushrooms really add no flavor. Dried mushrooms are great to keep in the pantry as they are easy to rehydrate and a little bit goes a long way.

Sambal Oelek Ground Fresh Chili Paste

This is a refrigerated chili paste that I use frequently in lieu of crushed red pepper flakes. The flavor of the Sambal Oelek is very pure and doesn't interfere or fight with other flavors in the recipes; instead, it adds a nice and pure chili flavor. Sambal Oelek can be used in any dish, where you want to add just a touch of heat or more heat. It can be added after cooking, too, so each person can decide if they want to add any extra heat to their meal.

Fish Sauce

This condiment adds tons of flavor to recipes. I suggest always having a bottle in your refrigerator. Only a very small amount is needed. Don't let the name fool you; there will not be a fishy taste as long as you only use a small amount. Be warned: don't put your nose to the bottle. I recommend Three Crabs Fish Sauce, which is made in Thailand, and Red Boat Fish Sauce, which is made in Vietnam.

Homemade Bone Broth

Not included in this book but found on my blog are recipes for my homemade bone broth recipes (chicken, beef, pork, etc.). Many of my recipes call for chicken broth. I suggest freezing the broth in 1 cup (240 ml) containers or Foodsaver bags (page 9). A good refrigerator must-have item is a jar of quality chicken base, which comes in handy when out of homemade broth. Check my blog for the brands that I recommend and use.

Pot-in-Pot Meals

The Pot-in-Pot method refers to placing another pot inside your cooking pot on top of a trivet to prepare a dish. It is also used to cook a second item at the same time as the food cooking in the cooking pot. For any recipe where you want to add rice, make sure the pressure cooking time is between 4 and 8 minutes. Any shorter than that and your rice will be hard; longer than that, and the rice will overcook. Potatoes can handle a longer cooking time. For 4 to 8 minutes, dice the potatoes into 1-inch (2.5 cm) cubes; for a longer cook time, use larger chunks of potatoes.

Freezer Meals

Freezer meals are in demand. We all have busy lives and sometimes just want a hot meal, and fast. A good tip is to buy large amounts of meat and chicken when on sale at the grocery store, and then look at some of your favorite recipes that require marinating time. Make the marinades, divide the meat and marinades into freezer bags, and pop them in the freezer—a Foodsaver (right) comes in handy for this. In the morning, pull out a package of meat and place it in the refrigerator. When you get home from work or errands, you are ready to cook, without any preparation.

Food Processor

A good food processor is a must-have for every kitchen. For many of my recipes, and to make your lives easier, I have incorporated the use of a food processor. In many cases, all ingredients can be chopped at once. It is also helpful to use in recipes with ground meat, as you can easily incorporate the ingredients and the meat stays together better.

Stainless Steel Trivets/Steam Rack

I suggest purchasing both a short-legged and tall-legged trivet. These are used inside the cooking pot for Pot-in-Pot Meals (above). The trivet is placed over the food in the cooking pot and then a casserole dish or other pan is placed on the trivet.

It is also used for when you want to cook using a casserole dish or baking pan. When using a trivet in the pressure cooker to only cook the food in a casserole or other dish, make sure at least 1½ cups (350 ml) of water is in the cooking pot. If using the Pot-in-Pot method (left) to cook a second recipe, there is no need to add additional water to the cooking pot, as the recipe being cooked in the cooking pot will have enough liquid for the pot to come to pressure.

Steamer Basket

This is another recommended kitchen essential that fits in the pressure cooking pot and has a myriad of uses, such as hard-boiling eggs (page 21).

Pans

A set of pressure-cooker stainless steel, stackable pans is a must-have. One pan can be used on top of a trivet for cooking rice or potatoes with my Pot-in-Pot method (left). They are also great for making a layer cake. A 6-inch (15 cm) PushPan is great to have on hand for making cheesecake and lasagna.

Aluminum Foil

This common household item is great for making a sling to easily lift pans and dishes in and out of the cooking pot. You can also buy a silicone sling.

Foodsaver

A Foodsaver is handy for buying meat when it is on sale and dividing it up, along with marinade, and popping it in the freezer for Freezer Meals (left). When you plan to cook, place one of the bags in the refrigerator to defrost and the meat will marinate as it defrosts.

Silicone Sealing Rings

The silicone ring that comes with the pressure cooker will become discolored and hold on to strong, savory smells. I suggest purchasing a few of them and marking and using them for savory, regular, and sweet dishes.

SEASONINGS, SAUCES, AND MORE

TOG HOUSE SEASONING

PREP TIME: 5 MIN. YIELD: 4.5 OUNCES (126 G)

2 tablespoons (30 ml) salt
3 tablespoons (45 ml) celery salt
1 teaspoon celery seed
¼ cup (50 g) sugar
1 teaspoon paprika
½ teaspoon ground turmeric
½ teaspoon onion powder
½ teaspoon garlic powder
½ teaspoon cornstarch or potato starch

Mix together all the ingredients and store in an airtight container.

SEAFOOD SEASONING

PREP TIME: 10 MIN. YIELD: 4 OUNCES (113 G)

5 teaspoons ground celery seed
5 teaspoons dry mustard
3 teaspoons ground bay leaves
4 teaspoons parsley flakes
1 tablespoon (15 ml) sea salt
1½ teaspoons paprika
¾ teaspoon allspice
¾ teaspoon ground ginger
½ teaspoon freshly ground black pepper
⅜ teaspoon ground cardamom
⅜ teaspoon ground cinnamon
¼ teaspoon ground white pepper
¼ teaspoon crushed red pepper flakes

Mix together all the ingredients and store in an airtight container.

TACO SEASONING

PREP TIME: 5 MIN. YIELD: 1.5 OUNCES (43 G)

1 tablespoon (15 ml) mild chili powder
¼ teaspoon garlic powder
¼ teaspoon onion powder
¼ teaspoon dried minced onion
1½ teaspoons ground cumin
¼ teaspoon dried oregano
½ teaspoon paprika
Pinch cayenne pepper
¾ teaspoon sea salt, or to taste
½ teaspoon freshly ground black pepper, or to taste

Mix together all the ingredients and store in an airtight container.

GARLIC-GINGER PASTE

PREP TIME: 10 MIN. YIELD: 8 OUNCES (227 G)

4 ounces (113 g) fresh ginger, peeled
4 ounces (113 g) garlic, peeled
1 to 2 teaspoons water
Pinch sea salt

1. Place all the ingredients into a blender or food processor and process until slightly smooth.

2. Store in the refrigerator in a covered glass vessel, such as a Mason jar, or freeze for later use (see TOG Tip!).

🩶 **TOG TIP!**
Remember to use water as the liquid and not oil. The combination of garlic's low acidity level and oil's lack of oxygen may cause botulism, which is toxic. If you want to store larger portions of the paste, freeze individual servings in ice cube trays or baby food molds in a covered ice cube tray. When you need some paste, just pop out a cube or two.

SPAGHETTI SAUCE FOR PASTA

PREP TIME: 10 MIN. COOK TIME: 10 MIN.
YIELD: 6 SERVINGS

1 tablespoon (15 ml) olive oil
2 pounds (907 g) mild or hot Italian sausage,
  casings removed (optional)
1 onion, chopped (optional)
3 or 4 garlic cloves, minced
2 cans (15 ounces, or 425 g, each) tomato sauce
1 can (28 ounces, or 794 g) diced tomatoes
1 can (6 ounces, or 170 g) tomato paste
½ cup (120 ml) red wine (a good cabernet)
½ cup (120 ml) water
1 tablespoon (2 g) dried basil
2 teaspoons dried parsley flakes
2 teaspoons packed light brown sugar
2 teaspoons sea salt
2 teaspoons fennel seeds, crushed
¼ to ½ teaspoon red pepper flakes,
¼ teaspoon freshly ground black pepper
Parmesan rind

1. On your pressure cooker, select Sauté or
    Browning and fully preheat the cooking pot.

2. Add the olive oil to the cooking pot and then
    the sausage (if using). Cook the sausage until
    brown, breaking it up with a spoon as you
    cook.

3. Add the onion, garlic, tomato sauce, tomatoes,
    tomato paste, red wine, water, basil, parsley,
    brown sugar, sea salt, fennel seeds, red pepper
    flakes, black pepper, and cheese rind.

4. Lock the lid and close the pressure valve. Cook
    for 10 minutes on High Pressure. When the
    beep sounds, wait 15 minutes, then release the
    remaining pressure.

TZATZIKI SAUCE

PREP TIME: 10 MIN. YIELD: 1 CUP (230 G)

4 ounces (113 g) cucumber, peeled, cored,
  and roughly chopped
1 teaspoon kosher salt
1 cup homemade yogurt cheese
  (strained Greek yogurt; see TOG Tip!)
1 garlic clove
1 teaspoon dill weed
1 teaspoon True Lemon or 1 tablespoon lemon
  juice
Pinch freshly ground black pepper
3 fresh mint leaves

1. Sprinkle the chopped cucumber with the
    kosher salt, then place it in a paper towel
    and squeeze out the water.

2. Add all the ingredients to the bowl of a
    food processor and process until smooth.
    Taste and adjust seasonings to your liking.

💙 **TOG TIP!**

*There's no need to buy yogurt cheese. Use my
Greek Yogurt recipe (page 24) and strain the
yogurt for at least 1 day. You will end up with
yogurt cheese.*

SWEET 'N SOUR SAUCE

PREP TIME: 5 MIN. COOK TIME: 10 MIN.
YIELD: 4 SERVINGS

½ cup (100 g) sugar
5 tablespoons (70 g) ketchup
½ cup (120 ml) seasoned rice vinegar
1 tablespoon (15 ml) low-sodium soy sauce
½ teaspoon garlic powder
¼ teaspoon sea salt

1. In a medium saucepan over medium-high heat, whisk together all the ingredients for about 5 minutes.

2. Turn the heat to the lowest setting and simmer, uncovered, for 5 minutes.

PICO DE GALLO

PREP TIME: 15 MIN. YIELD: 3 CUPS (770 G)

1½ pounds (680 g) fresh, ripe, firm Roma tomatoes
8 ounces (227 g) red onion (diced)
2 ounces (60 g) jalapeño pepper
  (seeds removed/diced)
1½ teaspoons kosher salt, or more to taste
  (see TOG Tip!)
2 tablespoons (8 g) fresh cilantro leaves, chopped
2 key limes

1. Cut the tomatoes in half and remove the mesocarp (soft interior). Dice the tomatoes and place them on a paper towel to remove excess moisture. Dice the onions a bit smaller than tomatoes. Remove the stem and seeds, and finely dice the jalapeño pepper.

2. Add the tomatoes, onion, and jalapeño to a large bowl. Squeeze the limes over the mixture and sprinkle on the salt. Add the cilantro and mix it through.

♥ TOG TIP!
Kosher salt is half as salty as sea salt, so make sure you are using kosher salt.

ORANGE-CRANBERRY SAUCE

PREP TIME: 5 MIN. COOK TIME: 5 MIN.
YIELD: 8 SERVINGS

1 pound (454 g) fresh cranberries, rinsed and drained
1 cup (240 ml) orange juice
1 cup demerara sugar (substitute maple syrup, white sugar, or any sugar alternative)
1 teaspoon fresh ginger, grated (optional)
1 teaspoon ground cinnamon
1 cinnamon stick
1 teaspoon orange zest

1. Add the cranberries to the pressure cooker cooking pot, followed by the orange juice, sugar, ginger (if using), and cinnamon.

2. Lock the lid and close the pressure valve. Cook for 5 minutes on High Pressure. (The longer you cook, the more the cranberries break apart. To keep them relatively whole, cook for 5 to 7 minutes. For a more saucelike consistency, cook for 8 minutes.) When the beep sounds, wait 10 minutes, then release the remaining pressure.

3. For a thicker sauce, simmer until desired consistency. Mix in the orange zest. The sauce will thicken as it cools.

BERRY COMPOTE

PREP TIME: 5 MIN. COOK TIME: 1 MIN.
YIELD: 4 CUPS (1.3 KG)

1 pound (454 g) fresh berries (such as strawberries blueberries, blackberries, boysenberries), trimmed and cut in half
1 pound (454 g) fresh blueberries
¼ cup (50 g) sugar
2 teaspoons orange juice (or lemon juice)
Vanilla bean
Whole nutmeg
Ground cinnamon

1. Add the fruit to the pressure cooker cooking pot. Sprinkle with the sugar and let sit for 20 minutes. Add a little squeeze of orange juice.

2. Lock the lid and close the pressure valve. Cook for 1 minute on High Pressure. When the beep sounds, allow a 15-minute natural pressure release.

3. The compote will thicken as it cools.

🤍 TOG TIP!

Peaches, nectarines, or cherries will work, so use whatever you love. Frozen fruit will work too but will produce extra liquid. For a thicker compote, make a cornstarch slurry and simmer to thicken.

MASHED POTATOES

PREP TIME: 5 MIN. COOK TIME: 5 MIN. YIELD: 6 SERVINGS

1½ cups (350 ml) water, for the cooking pot
2 pounds Yukon Gold potatoes (or potato type of choice), peeled and quartered
1 cup (240 ml) milk or cream
2 teaspoons sea salt
¼ cup (60 g) salted butter, plus more butter for topping (optional)
Fresh or dried chives, for garnishing (optional)

1. Add the water to the pressure cooker cooking pot. Place the potatoes in a steamer basket and place the basket in the cooking pot.

2. Lock the lid and close the pressure valve. Cook for 7 minutes on High Pressure. When the beep sounds, wait 10 minutes, then release the remaining pressure.

3. Remove the potatoes from the pressure cooker and transfer to a large bowl. With a fork or potato masher, mash the potatoes until they are smashed.

4. Add the milk and continue mashing or whipping. Add the salt and continue mashing. Add the butter last and continue mashing or whipping, until desired texture is reached.

5. Taste and adjust the seasonings if needed. Top with the chives and a pat of butter, if desired.

BREAKFAST

FROSTED MINI FRITTATAS

Blueberries and Cream Oats

TROPICAL OATS

ORANGE-CRANBERRY FRENCH TOAST

Jalapeño Popper

SOUTHERN–STYLE GRITS

HARDBOILED EGGS AND YOGURT

Frosted Mini Frittatas

A frittata is basically an omelet or a crustless quiche with added meat and/or veggies. The eggs are whipped to incorporate air, yielding a fluffier result. Design your own individual mini for a grab-and-go breakfast.

Butter, for greasing the jars

7 large eggs

2 tablespoons (30 ml) heavy or whipping cream

½ teaspoon TOG House Seasoning (page 10)

½ cup (weight varies) mixed vegetables (such as raw, finely diced onions, mushrooms, asparagus, spinach, kale, and/or cooked, chopped potatoes)

4 ounces (113 g) cheese of choice, shredded or diced, plus more for "frosting"

4 ounces (113 g) meat (such as crisped bacon or cooked ham or sausage), diced

1 cup (240 ml) water, for the cooking pot

1 scallion, diced

1. Generously grease 4 half-pint wide-mouth (240 ml) Mason jars with butter (see TOG Tip!).

2. In a large bowl, whisk together the eggs, cream, and house seasoning until whipped. Evenly divide the egg mixture among the jars.

3. In a medium bowl, combine the vegetables, cheese, and meat. Evenly divide the mixture among the jars.

4. Place a stainless-steel trivet into the pressure cooker cooking pot and add the water to the pot. Place the Mason jars on the trivet.

5. Lock the lid and close the pressure valve. Cook for 4 minutes on High Pressure. When the beep sounds, wait 10 minutes, then release the remaining pressure.

6. Remove the lid and "frost" the frittatas with the extra grated cheese. Replace the lid and let sit for 1 minute. Garnish with scallion before serving.

♥ **TOG TIP!**

If you use 4-ounce (120 ml) jars, stack them in two layers and cook for 3 minutes on High Pressure.

Blueberries and Cream Steel-Cut Oats

PREP: 10 MIN.
COOK: 10 MIN.
YIELD: 4 SERVINGS

Healthy with a little sweetness, these steel-cut oats will stick to your ribs. Pop everything into your pressure cooker, go get ready for your day, and come back to a hot breakfast.

1 tablespoon (15 ml) coconut oil
1 cup (176 g) steel-cut oats
1½ cups (360 ml) water
1 cup (240 ml) milk
½ cup (120 ml) cream or half-and-half, plus more for serving
¾ cup (120 g) dried blueberries (see TOG Tip!)
2 tablespoons (30 ml) coconut sugar
1 tablespoon (15 ml) chia seeds
1 teaspoon vanilla extract
Pinch sea salt
½ cup (75 g) fresh blueberries

1. On your pressure cooker, select Sauté or Browning and fully heat the cooking pot.

2. Melt the coconut oil in the pressure cooker.

3. Add the oats and toast for about 3 minutes, stirring constantly.

4. Stir in the water, milk, cream, dried blueberries, coconut sugar, chia seeds, vanilla, and sea salt.

5. Lock the lid and close the pressure valve. Cook for 10 minutes on High Pressure. When the beep sounds, wait 10 minutes, then release the remaining pressure.

6. Remove the lid, stir, and serve topped with more cream and fresh blueberries.

🤍 **TOG TIP!**
Dried cranberries, strawberries, mangoes, or peaches can be used in place of the dried blueberries.

Tropical Coconut-Mango Steel-Cut Oats

PREP: 10 MIN.
COOK: 10 MIN.
YIELD: 4 SERVINGS

Creamy, sweet, and chewy, this hearty breakfast will keep you full until lunch. Easy to make ahead and reheat, too, this recipe has everything you want in a hot breakfast.

1 tablespoon (15 ml) coconut oil

1 cup (176 g) steel-cut oats

1 can (13.5 ounces, or 400 ml) canned unsweetened coconut milk (not the drinking type)

1¼ cups (300 ml) water

4 ounces (115 g) dried mango, diced

2 tablespoons (30 ml) coconut sugar

1 teaspoon vanilla extract

Pinch salt

Fresh mango slices, for serving

Coconut cream, for serving

Coconut flakes, for serving

1. On your pressure cooker, select Sauté or Browning and fully heat the cooking pot.

2. Melt the coconut oil in the pressure cooker.

3. Add the oats and toast for about 3 minutes, stirring constantly.

4. Add the coconut milk, water, dried mango, coconut sugar, vanilla, and salt.

5. Lock the lid and close the pressure valve. Cook for 10 minutes on High Pressure. When the beep sounds, wait 10 minutes, then release the remaining pressure.

6. Remove the lid and stir the oats well to combine—they will be a bit runny at first. To thicken them, give them a good stir and let them sit for a few minutes. For an even thicker consistency, select Sauté or Browning and cook until it reaches desired consistency.

7. Serve in bowls topped with fresh mango slices, a drizzle of coconut cream, and a sprinkle of coconut flakes.

♥ **TOG TIP!**

You can also top this oatmeal with almonds, granola, agave, honey, or maple syrup.

Southern-Style Cheesy Grits

Imagine enjoying grits, without all the stirring and pot watching.
My cheesy grits are truly a Southern breakfast gem.

PREP: 5 MIN.
COOK: 10 MIN.
YIELD: 4 SERVINGS

2 tablespoons (30 ml) bacon grease,
  coconut oil, or other oil
1 cup (140 g) stone-ground grits (not
  instant)
3 cups (720 ml) water
1¾ cups (400 ml) cream, half-
  and-half, or milk
4 ounces (115 g) Cheddar cheese, diced
2 to 3 tablespoons (28 to 42 g) salted
  butter, plus more for garnishing
2 teaspoons sea salt

1. On your pressure cooker, select Sauté or Browning and fully heat the pot.

2. Add the bacon grease and grits, and toast for 3 minutes, stirring constantly. Turn off the pressure cooker.

3. Add the water, cream, butter, and salt, and stir to combine.

4. Lock the lid and close the pressure valve. Cook for 10 minutes on High Pressure. When the beep sounds, wait 15 minutes, then release the remaining pressure.

5. Remove the lid and stir the grits. They will thicken as they cool.

6. Serve with a pat of butter on top.

Hard-Boiled Eggs

PREP: 5 MIN.
COOK: 2 MIN.

From the day I posted my "2-minute-set-and-forget-it method" on my blog, it became the most talked about hard-boiled egg method for the pressure cooker and quickly revolutionized the way people cook their eggs.

1 cup (240 ml) water, for the cooking pot
Large eggs (as many as you like
   and can fit)

1. Add the water to the pressure cooker cooking pot.

2. Place the eggs in a steamer basket or on a trivet in the cooking pot.

3. Lock the lid and close the pressure valve. Cook for 2 minutes on High Pressure. When the beep sounds, allow a natural pressure release. Open when you feel like it (within reason); 15 minutes is good. If you plan to be away from the cooker for longer than 15 minutes while the pressure releases, reduce the cooking time to 1 minute.

4. Peel the eggs if using immediately, or refrigerate, unpeeled, for up to 1 week.

Jalapeño Popper Soufflé

PREP: 20 MIN.
COOK: 15–20 MIN.
YIELD: 4–6 SERVINGS

I grew up in South Florida eating Spanish *tortilla*—eggs, potatoes, *sofrito*, and cheese—cooked on the stove. This recipe is my Tex-Mex version.

Soufflé

Butter, for greasing the casserole dish
1½ ounces (43 g) Cheddar cheese, shredded
1½ ounces (43 g) Monterey Jack cheese, shredded
¼ teaspoon hot sauce
¼ teaspoon dried oregano
Pinch ground cumin
6 jalapeño peppers, stemmed
6 large eggs
¼ cup (60 ml) heavy cream
¼ cup (60 g) cream cheese
½ teaspoon sea salt
¼ teaspoon freshly ground black pepper
1½ cups (355 ml) water, for the cooking pot

Topping

¼ cup (30 g) seasoned bread crumbs
¼ cup (30 g) Cheddar cheese, grated

♥ TOG TIP!

If using a stainless steel dish instead of a ceramic casserole dish, reduce the cooking time by 5 minutes.

1. **To make the soufflé:** Generously grease a 7- to 8-inch (18 to 20 cm) casserole dish with butter (see TOG Tip!).

2. In a small bowl, combine the Cheddar and Monterey Jack cheeses, hot sauce, oregano, and cumin.

3. Cut a lengthwise slit into each jalapeño, being careful not to cut all the way through, and remove the seeds and ribs. Carefully stuff each jalapeño with the cheese mixture and place them into the prepared casserole dish.

4. In a heavy-duty blender or food processor, combine the eggs, heavy cream, cream cheese, sea salt, and black pepper. Process until frothy. Pour the egg mixture into the casserole dish over the peppers. Cover the dish.

5. Place a stainless-steel trivet into the pressure cooker cooking pot and add the water to the pot. Place the casserole dish on the trivet.

6. Lock the lid and close the pressure valve. Cook for 20 minutes on High Pressure. When the beep sounds, wait 10 minutes, then release the remaining pressure.

7. **To make the topping:** In a small bowl, combine the bread crumbs and Cheddar cheese. Sprinkle the topping over the soufflé, and place the dish under the broiler until bubbly.

Yogurt and Greek-Style Yogurt

PREP: 1 HOUR
COOK: 6–10 HOURS
YIELD: 12 SERVINGS

This delicious, thick, and creamy yogurt recipe is for pressure cookers with the Yogurt function. Strain the yogurt to make it Greek-style.

1 gallon (3.8 L) whole milk (see TOG Tips!)

2 tablespoons (30 g) yogurt "starter" (any yogurt made with milk and live/active cultures only)

♥ TOG TIPS!

Fat-free, 2%, or 1% milk can be used, but the yogurt will not be as thick as that made with whole milk.

For ½ gallon (1.9 L) milk, use 1 tablespoon (15 g) starter. All instructions remain the same.

For tangy or tart yogurt, increase the time to 9, 10, or more hours. For less tart, mild yogurt, decrease the time to 5 to 7 hours. The longer you incubate, the tangier the yogurt becomes.

To strain for Greek yogurt, use a yogurt or regular strainer lined with cheesecloth or butter muslin.

1. Make the yogurt (not under pressure): Pour the milk into the cooking pot. Cover the pot with the lid and close the pressure valve. Select Yogurt and Adjust until it says "Boil." The boil cycle takes about 45 minutes; every 15 minutes or so, remove the lid and whisk the milk.

2. When the beep sounds, remove the lid, whisk, and check the temperature with an instant-read thermometer. If the temperature has not reached 180°F to 185°F (82°C to 85°C), select Sauté or Browning (Low), and whisk continuously until the temperature has been reached.

3. When the correct temperature is reached (180°F to 185°F, or 82°C to 85°C), remove the cooking pot from the cooker and place it in a sink full of cold water. Cool the milk to between 95°F and 110°F (35°C and 43°C), whisking often. This takes about 10 minutes.

4. Transfer ½ cup (120 ml) of the cooled milk to a small bowl and whisk in the starter. Pour the milk-starter mixture back into the cooking pot and whisk thoroughly to combine. Place the cooking pot back into the pressure cooker and re-cover with the lid.

5. Select Yogurt. The display screen will default to 8:00 (select Yogurt again or select Adjust, if necessary; see TOG Tips!).

6. If you'd like to make Greek-style yogurt, strain the yogurt in the refrigerator for at least 2 hours (see TOG Tips!). Your whey should be translucent/clear.

Orange-Cranberry French Toast

PREP: 30 MIN.
COOK: 20 MIN.
YIELD: 6 SERVINGS

I usually make this dish the day after Thanksgiving, but it is also great for Christmas Day, or any time of the year!

Crumble

2 tablespoons (28 g) salted butter, frozen
¼ cup (50 g) packed light brown sugar

French Toast

1 loaf challah, cut into 1-inch (2.5 cm) cubes
6 large eggs, beaten
1 cup (240 ml) whole milk
2 tablespoons (30 ml) sugar
1 teaspoon vanilla extract
¼ teaspoon grated orange zest
⅛ teaspoon kosher salt
2 tablespoons (28 g) salted butter, melted
1 cup (280 g) Orange-Cranberry Sauce (page 12)
1 cup (240 ml) water, for the cooking pot

Topping

½ cup (140 g) Orange-Cranberry Sauce (page 12)
¼ cup (30 g) confectioners' sugar

Serving

Walnuts, pecans, Grape-Nuts cereal, or maple syrup, for serving

♥ **TOG TIP!**
Other fruit compotes, such as blueberry or strawberry can be used in place of the orange-cranberry sauce.

1. **To make the crumble:** In a small bowl, grate the frozen butter. Add the brown sugar, then gently combine with a fork to form a crumble. Set aside.

2. **To make the French toast:** Place the challah cubes in a medium bowl.

3. In a small bowl, whisk together the eggs, milk, sugar, vanilla, orange zest, and kosher salt, until frothy. Pour the egg mixture over the bread and mix thoroughly, making sure the bread is well coated. Refrigerate for 20 minutes, mixing in any egg that has fallen to the bottom of the bowl.

4. Add the melted butter to a 1½-quart (1.4 L) casserole dish and tilt to coat the bottom and sides. Add half the bread mixture to the prepared dish and press down. Spoon the orange-cranberry sauce over the bread. Top with the remaining bread and sprinkle the crumble over the top.

5. Place a stainless-steel trivet into the cooking pot and add the water to the pot. Using a foil sling, lower the casserole dish onto the trivet.

6. Lock the lid and close the pressure valve. Cook for 20 minutes on High Pressure. When the beep sounds, wait 5 minutes, then release the remaining pressure.

7. **To make the topping:** In a small saucepan over low heat, warm the orange-cranberry sauce. Pour it over the warm French toast and sprinkle with confectioners' sugar.

8. Serve topped with nuts, Grape-Nuts, or maple syrup as desired.

CHICKEN
DINNERS

SPICY CHICKEN BOW TIES

Enchiladas

POLYNESIAN • **HONEY BOURBON**
SAN BEI JI • CREAMY TUSCAN
HONEY GARLIC • *Rojo Fiesta*
AND **BRUSCHETTA**
CHICKEN

Spicy Chicken Bow Ties

This succulent chicken-breast recipe has a spicy, tangy, cheesy sauce—not your mother's mac and cheese!

PREP: 15 MIN.
COOK: 3 MIN.
YIELD: 4 SERVINGS

1½ pounds (680 g) white chicken meat, cut into 2-inch (5 cm) chunks

8 ounces (225 g) bow tie pasta

1¾ cups (14 ounces, or 425 ml) chicken broth

3 celery ribs, diced

1 small onion, diced

½ red bell pepper, diced

½ orange bell pepper, diced

½ cup (120 ml) hot sauce

3 tablespoons (42 g) salted butter

1 tablespoon (15 ml) distilled white vinegar

2 teaspoons Worcestershire sauce

2 teaspoons sea salt

1 teaspoon packed light brown sugar

¼ teaspoon freshly ground black pepper

¼ teaspoon dried parsley

⅛ teaspoon garlic powder

⅛ teaspoon onion powder

½ cup (115 g) Greek Yogurt (page 24; see TOG Tip!)

4 ounces (115 g) sharp Cheddar cheese, shredded

4 ounces (115 g) Jarlsberg cheese, shredded (any type of Swiss cheese can be substituted)

4 ounces (115 g) feta or cotija cheese

½ cup (50 g) scallions, chopped

1. In the pressure cooker cooking pot, combine the chicken, pasta, chicken broth, celery, onion, red and orange bell peppers, hot sauce, butter, vinegar, Worcestershire sauce, sea salt, brown sugar, black pepper, parsley, garlic powder, and onion powder.

2. Lock the lid and close the pressure valve. Cook for 3 minutes on High Pressure. When the beep sounds, wait 10 minutes and release the remaining pressure.

3. Remove the lid and stir in the yogurt, cheeses, and scallions, stirring until the cheeses melt.

♥ **TOG TIP!**

No Greek yogurt? Substitute 4 ounces (113 g) cream cheese mixed with 1 tablespoon (15 ml) vinegar.

Chicken Enchiladas Suizas

PREP: 30 MIN.
COOK: 2 MIN.
YIELD: 4–6 SERVINGS

In 1990, I lost 130 pounds (60 kg) by counting calories. Frozen chicken enchilada suizas were a treat for me, and I would sometimes save up my calories just so I could have a decent-size dinner. Those days are gone, and these enchiladas with homemade salsa verde are so much better.

1½ teaspoons salt

½ teaspoon freshly ground black pepper

½ teaspoon chili powder

½ teaspoon ground cumin

1½ pounds (680 g) boneless, skinless chicken breast, fat trimmed, cut into 2-inch (5 cm) chunks

1 tablespoon (15 ml) extra-virgin olive oil, plus more for frying tortillas

1 tablespoon (14 g) salted butter

¼ cup (60 ml) chicken broth

2 pounds (907 g) tomatillos, husked

2 serrano chiles (green), stemmed

2 Guerito chiles (yellowish green), stemmed

1 small onion, peeled and halved

3 garlic cloves

½ bunch fresh cilantro

12 white corn tortillas

1½ cups (336 g) Mexican crema, crème fraîche, or half sour cream and half heavy cream

10 ounces (280 g) Oaxaca cheese, shredded (see TOG Tips!)

4 ounces (115 g) cotija cheese, crumbled

♥ TOG TIPS!

You can substitute Monterey Jack or mozzarella for the Oaxaca cheese.

One-half of the cotija cheese can be rolled inside the tortillas with the chicken in step 10, if desired.

1. In a medium bowl, combine the salt, black pepper, chili powder, and cumin. Add the chicken chunks and toss to coat.

2. Add the olive oil, butter, chicken chunks, chicken broth, tomatillos, serrano and Guerito chiles, and onion to the cooking pot.

3. Lock the lid and close the pressure valve. Cook for 2 minutes on High Pressure. When the beep sounds, wait 5 minutes, then release the remaining pressure.

4. Remove the lid and transfer the chicken to a bowl. Shred it well with 2 forks.

5. Transfer the vegetables and liquid from the cooking pot to a heavy-duty blender and add the garlic and cilantro to make salsa verde. Process until smooth. Alternatively, use an immersion blend to blend the ingredients in the pot.

6. Preheat the oven to 350°F (180°C).

7. Pour half the salsa verde from the blender into a 9 x 13-inch (23 x 33 cm) baking dish.

8. In a large skillet over medium-high heat, heat a drop of olive oil.

9. Add a few tortillas at a time to the hot oil, adding more oil as necessary, and flip them over, frying for 15 seconds per side. Transfer to a paper towel to drain. Don't skip this step—lightly frying the tortillas makes them pliable and easier to roll.

10. Place one tortilla at a time on a flat work surface and add about ⅓ cup (50 g) shredded chicken. Roll up the tortilla and place it seam side down in the baking dish. Repeat with the remaining tortillas and chicken.

11. Pour the remaining salsa verde over the enchiladas. Drizzle the Mexican crema over the top and cover with the Oaxaca cheese. Bake for 30 minutes, or until the cheese is melted and bubbly.

12. Crumble the cotija over the enchiladas and serve (see TOG Tips!).

Notes

Polynesian Chicken

Sweet and tangy, this chicken dish will transport you to a luau.

PREP: 20 MIN.
COOK: 5 MIN.
YIELD: 4–6 SERVINGS

Sauce

½ cup (120 ml) chicken broth
½ cup (120 ml) unsweetened pineapple juice
½ cup (120 ml) seasoned rice vinegar
¼ cup (65 g) tomato paste
¼ cup (60 ml) soy sauce
¼ cup (50 g) packed dark brown sugar
2 tablespoons (30 g) Dijon mustard
2 tablespoons (30 ml) red wine vinegar
2 tablespoons (30 ml) Worcestershire sauce
2 tablespoons (30 ml) vegetable or canola oil
1½-inch (4 cm) piece fresh ginger, peeled and grated
½ teaspoon red pepper flakes

Chicken

2 pounds (907 g) boneless, skinless chicken breast, cut into 3-inch (7.5 cm) chunks and patted dry
1 teaspoon sea salt
¼ teaspoon freshly ground black pepper
¼ cup (45 g) potato starch
1 tablespoon (15 ml) extra-virgin olive oil
1 large orange bell pepper, cut into 2-inch (5 cm) chunks
¼ cup (40 g) onion, roughly chopped
14 ounces (395 g) jasmine rice, rinsed until the water runs clear
1¾ cups (425 ml) water
8 ounces (225 g) fresh snow peas
1 cup (165 g) pineapple chunks

Garnish

1 small bell pepper (any color), diced

1. **To make the sauce:** In a large bowl, add all the sauce ingredients and whisk to combine. Set aside.

2. **To make the chicken:** In another large bowl, season the chicken with the sea salt and black pepper. Add the potato starch and toss to coat.

3. On your pressure cooker, select Sauté or Browning and fully heat the cooking pot.

4. Add the oil to the cooking pot.

5. Shake off the excess potato starch from the chicken and place it in the cooking pot. Mix the chicken around the pot for 30 seconds to lightly brown.

6. Pour in the sauce and combine with the chicken, scraping up any browned bits from the bottom of the pot.

7. Stir in the bell pepper and onion. Place a tall-legged stainless-steel trivet over the chicken.

8. In a flat-bottom, stainless-steel pan, combine the rice and water. Place the pan on the trivet.

9. Lock the lid and close the pressure valve. Cook for 5 minutes on High Pressure. When the beep sounds, wait 10 minutes, then release the remaining pressure.

10. Remove the lid, rice, and trivet. Fluff the rice with a fork.

11. Stir in the snow peas and pineapple, and let sit until the snow peas have softened.

12. Serve the chicken over the rice, garnished with the diced bell pepper.

Honey Bourbon Chicken Wings

PREP: 15 MIN.
COOK: 5 MIN.
YIELD: 4 SERVINGS

These chicken wings are super easy to make, delicious, and can be on your table in about 30 minutes.

¾ cup (180 g) ketchup
½ cup (100 g) packed light brown sugar
¼ cup (40 g) onion, finely minced
2 garlic cloves, finely crushed
1 tablespoon (15 ml) liquid smoke
½ cup (120 ml) water
¼ cup (60 ml) bourbon
3 tablespoons (60 g) clover honey
2 teaspoons smoked paprika
1 teaspoon sea salt
½ teaspoon freshly ground black pepper
¼ teaspoon cayenne pepper
4 to 5 pounds (1.8 to 2.2 kg) chicken wing pieces

💙 **TOG TIP!**

If you don't feel like making homemade barbecue sauce, use a bottle of your favorite sauce instead. Add 1 cup (240 ml) water to your pressure cooker cooking pot with a steamer basket full of wings. Cook for 5 minutes on High Pressure. Once the pressure is released, crisp the wings as in step 5.

1. On your pressure cooker, select Sauté or Browning. In the pressure cooker cooking pot, combine the ketchup, brown sugar, onion, garlic, and liquid smoke. Cook for about 5 minutes, stirring, until the sauce starts to thicken. Turn off the pressure cooker.

2. Stir in the water, bourbon, honey, paprika, sea salt, black pepper, and cayenne pepper.

3. Carefully add the wings to the cooking pot and mix them into the sauce.

4. Lock the lid and close the pressure valve. Cook for 5 minutes on High Pressure. When the beep sounds, do a quick pressure release.

5. Remove the lid, and using tongs, carefully transfer the wings to a parchment paper–lined baking sheet or air fryer basket. If using an oven, place the wings on the middle rack and broil for 5 minutes per side. Remove the wings, slather on the sauce, and place back in the oven. Broil for 5 minutes more per side. If using an air fryer, place the wings in the basket and cook at 400°F (200°C) for 6 minutes. Remove the basket and dunk the wings in the thickened sauce in the pressure cooker. Return the wings to the air fryer and cook at to 400°F (200°C) for 6 minutes more.

6. While the wings crisp, turn the pressure cooker to Sauté or Browning and let the sauce thicken.

San Bei Ji
(Taiwanese Three-Cup Chicken)

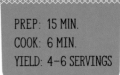

PREP: 15 MIN.
COOK: 6 MIN.
YIELD: 4–6 SERVINGS

This simple recipe, with few ingredients, produces very flavorful chicken, as the sauce cooks into the chicken. It is called Three-Cup Chicken for its three "sauces": soy, rice wine, and sesame oil.

¼ cup (60 ml) sesame oil

2 pounds (907 g) skin-on, bone-in chicken thighs (see TOG Tip!)

2-inch (5 cm) piece fresh ginger, peeled and thinly sliced

1 garlic head (about 12 to 15 cloves), peeled

3 large scallions, sliced into 1-inch (2.5 cm) pieces

1 or 2 dried Chinese or Thai red chiles

½ cup (120 ml) rice wine

1½ tablespoons (23 g) packed light brown sugar

¼ cup (60 ml) soy sauce

1½ cups (53 g) fresh Thai basil leaves

1 recipe Perfectly Cooked Pot-in Pot Rice (page 153; optional)

♥ TOG TIP!

If you prefer bite-size pieces, without skin and bones, use 2-inch (5 cm) chunks of chicken thighs. For step 2, instead of browning the chicken skin, skip to step 3 and then add the chicken chunks at step 5 after reducing the sauce. Cook for 4 minutes.

1. On your pressure cooker, select Sauté or Browning and fully heat the cooking pot.

2. Add the sesame oil to the pot and place the chicken in it, skin-side down. Brown the chicken until it begins to crisp. Transfer to a plate.

3. Add the ginger, garlic, scallions, and chiles to the oil in the pot. Sauté for 30 seconds.

4. Pour in the rice wine to deglaze the cooking pot, scraping up any browned bits from the bottom of the pot. Simmer for 1 minute.

5. Stir in the brown sugar and soy sauce. Simmer for 3 minutes to reduce and thicken the sauce. Return the chicken to the cooking pot.

6. If making the rice, place a tall-legged stainless-steel trivet into the pressure cooker cooking pot and place the pan of rice and broth (as instructed in the recipe on page 153) on it.

7. Lock the lid and close the pressure valve. Cook for 6 minutes on High Pressure. When the beep sounds, wait 10 minutes, then release the remaining pressure.

8. Remove the lid and select Sauté or Browning. Simmer the sauce to reduce further, about 5 minutes.

9. Stir in the Thai basil and serve over the rice (if using).

Honey Garlic Chicken

PREP: 10 MIN.
COOK: 5 MIN.
YIELD: 4 SERVINGS

Honey Garlic Chicken is a quick weeknight meal that can be on your table in about 30 minutes, including a side of rice.

¾ cup (180 g) ketchup
¾ cup (255 g) clover honey
½ cup (120 ml) low-sodium soy sauce
¼ cup (60 ml) water
3 tablespoons (30 g) garlic, minced
2 teaspoons Sambal Oelek Ground Fresh Chili Paste
3 pounds (1.3 kg) boneless, skinless chicken thighs, fat trimmed
2 tablespoons (30 ml) potato starch
1 recipe Perfectly Cooked Pot-in-Pot Rice (page 153; optional)

1. In your pressure cooker cooking pot, combine the ketchup, honey, soy sauce, water, garlic, and chili paste.

2. Add the chicken and stir to coat. Dredge the chicken through the potato starch and add it to the cooking pot.

3. If making the rice, place a tall-legged stainless-steel trivet into the pressure cooker cooking pot and place the pan of rice and broth (as instructed in the recipe on page 153) on it.

4. Lock the lid and close the pressure valve. Cook for 5 minutes on High Pressure. When the beep sounds, wait 10 minutes, then release the remaining pressure.

5. Remove the lid, rice, and trivet from the pot. Quickly cover the rice to finish steaming.

6. Select Sauté or Browning and bring the liquid to a boil, stirring constantly until the sauce thickens.

7. Serve over the rice (if using).

Bruschetta Chicken with Zoodles

PREP: 15 MIN.
COOK: 3 MIN.
YIELD: 4 SERVINGS

Enjoy this simple and healthy one-pot, low-carb, gluten-free meal with "zoodles" (zucchini noodles).

48 onces (1.4 kg) canned diced tomatoes, drained (see TOG Tips!)

1 garlic head, cloves peeled and minced

½ cup (80 g) red onion, diced

¼ cup (60 ml) extra-virgin olive oil

2 tablespoons (30 ml) balsamic vinegar

1 tablespoon (17 g) chicken base

½ teaspoon sea salt

¼ teaspoon freshly ground black pepper

4 chicken breasts, lightly pounded

⅔ cup (53 g) Parmesan cheese, freshly shredded

2 tablespoons (28 g) salted butter

½ cup (20 g) fresh basil leaves, chopped

2 zucchini, spiralized into zoodles (see TOG Tips!)

6 ounces (170 g) mozzarella cheese, thinly sliced

1. In the pressure cooker cooking pot, combine the tomatoes, garlic, onion, olive oil, vinegar, chicken base, salt, and pepper.

2. Add the chicken and Parmesan.

3. Lock the lid and close the pressure valve. Cook for 3 minutes on Low Pressure. When the beep sounds, wait 5 minutes, then release the remaining pressure.

4. Remove the lid and stir in the butter and basil.

5. Place the chicken on the zoodles. Lay the mozzarella slices over the chicken and spoon the hot bruschetta sauce over the top.

♥ **TOG TIPS!**

Fresh tomatoes can be used instead of canned.

Zoodles can be raw or added to the cooking pot after the pressure is released. The residual heat will cook them quickly.

Substitute pasta for zoodles, if desired.

Creamy Tuscan Garlic Chicken

PREP: 20 MIN.
COOK: 3 MIN.
YIELD: 4 SERVINGS

This meal is saucy and full of flavor, and perfect for low-carbers when served with zoodles (page 37). It is also delicious with pasta (see TOG Tip!).

1 teaspoon TOG House Seasoning (page 10)
1 tablespoon (15 ml) Italian seasoning
2 pounds (907 g) boneless, skinless chicken breast, halved and pounded ½ inch (13 mm) thick
¼ cup (45 g) potato starch
1 tablespoon (15 ml) extra-virgin olive oil
1½ tablespoons (23 g) salted butter
6 garlic cloves, minced
¼ cup (60 ml) dry sherry or dry white wine
¾ cup (175 ml) low-sodium chicken broth
¾ cup (175 ml) heavy or whipping cream, or to taste
1 cup (80 g) Asiago or Parmesan cheese, freshly shredded
¼ to ½ cup (14 to 27 g) sun-dried tomato strips
1½ cups (45 g) fresh spinach, roughly chopped

♥ TOG TIP!

To make Tuscan Garlic Chicken Pasta: After adding the chicken back into the pot in step 8, add 8 ounces (227 g) of linguine and 2 cups (475 ml) of water to the pot, then continue with the recipe.

1. In a small bowl, combine the house seasoning and Italian seasoning. Press the spices onto both sides of the chicken pieces.

2. Place the potato starch in a shallow bowl. Dredge the seasoned chicken in the starch. Shake off any excess starch and set aside.

3. On your pressure cooker, select Sauté or Browning and fully heat the cooking pot.

4. Add the olive oil and butter to the cooking pot.

5. Working in batches, add the chicken and sear for 5 seconds per side. Transfer the chicken to a plate.

6. Add the garlic to the cooking pot and sauté for 30 seconds.

7. Pour in the sherry and deglaze the cooking pot. Add the chicken broth, scraping up any browned bits from the bottom of the pot. Turn off the pressure cooker.

8. Return the chicken to the cooking pot.

9. Lock the lid and close the pressure valve. Cook for 3 minutes at High Pressure. When the beep sounds, slowly release all the pressure.

10. Remove the lid, select Sauté or Browning, and stir in the cream. Simmer for 2 minutes.

11. Add the cheese, sundried tomatoes, and spinach. Simmer until the spinach wilts.

Rojo Fiesta Chicken

A party in your mouth, this dump-and-go meal takes little effort.

PREP: 10 MIN.
COOK: 4 MIN.
YIELD: 4 SERVINGS

2 pounds (907 g) boneless, skinless, chicken breasts (see TOG Tips!)

1 pound (454 g) diced tomatoes (canned or fresh)

1 medium yellow onion, seeded and diced

1 cup (250 g) barbecue sauce, regular or sugar-free

2 garlic cloves, minced

2 jalapeño peppers, diced

2 tablespoons (30 ml) freshly squeezed lime juice

1 tablespoon (15 ml) freshly squeezed lemon juice

1 tablespoon (15 ml) kosher salt

1 teaspoon Sambal Oelek Ground Fresh Chili Paste

¼ cup (4 g) fresh cilantro leaves, chopped

1. Add all the ingredients, except the cilantro, to the pressure cooker cooking pot.

2. Lock the lid and close the pressure value. Cook for 4 minutes on High Pressure. When the beep sounds, wait 10 minutes, then release the remaining pressure.

3. Remove the lid and transfer the chicken to a plate. Select Sauté or Browning and simmer to thicken the sauce. Stir in the cilantro.

4. Plate the chicken and serve with the sauce.

♥ TOG TIPS!

Depending on the type of chicken you use, the following cooking times apply:

- *chicken wings: 5 minutes*
- *bone-in, skin-on thighs and legs: 8 minutes*
- *bone-in, skin-on chicken breasts: 7 minutes*
- *boneless, skinless thighs and legs: 5 minutes.*

If using chicken with skin, brown the chicken in an air fryer or under the broiler.

PORK DINNERS

LOW-COUNTRY PULLED PORK

Pork Carnitas • LECHON ASADO

BALSAMIC-SPICED APPLE

PORK CHOPS IN GRAVY

ORANGE-GLAZED PORK

Shoyu Pork

AND VIETNAMESE MEATBALLS

Low-Country Pulled Pork

PREP: 1 DAY AHEAD
COOK: 40 MIN.
YIELD: 8 SERVINGS

This recipe is close to my heart and reminds me of my time in Charleston, South Carolina. Many weekends were spent with good friends relaxing on my porch, slow-cooking my famous pulled pork on the barbecue grill, and watching the ducks swim in the pond.

Coleslaw (made 1 day ahead)

1 large head cabbage, shredded
2 large carrots, shredded
¾ cup (175 g) mayonnaise
2 tablespoons (30 ml) sugar
1 tablespoon (15 ml) milk
1 tablespoon (15 ml) freshly squeezed lemon juice
1 tablespoon (15 ml) distilled white vinegar
1 teaspoon salt
½ teaspoon freshly ground black pepper

Rub

½ cup (100 g) packed dark brown sugar
⅓ cup (32 g) freshly ground black pepper
¼ cup (75 g) kosher salt
¼ cup (30 g) chili powder
¼ cup (28 g) ground cumin
¼ cup (36 g) hot dry mustard
3 tablespoons (25 g) paprika
2 tablespoons (30 ml) granulated garlic powder
2 tablespoons (30 ml) granulated onion powder
1 teaspoon cayenne pepper

♥ TOG TIPS!

When making the coleslaw as a stand-alone recipe, add 1 teaspoon celery seed, if desired.

You will have plenty of rub left over. Store any extra in an airtight container for use on beef, ribs, and chicken.

Mop Sauce

1 large Red Delicious apple, peeled and cored
1 cup (240 ml) distilled white vinegar
¾ cup (175 ml) beer
½ cup (100 g) packed dark brown sugar
½ cup (120 g) ketchup
3 tablespoons (45 g) spicy mustard
3 tablespoons (33 g) yellow mustard
2 tablespoons (30 ml) Worcestershire sauce
1 tablespoon (15 ml) freshly ground black pepper
1 tablespoon (15 ml) kosher salt

Pulled Pork

5 pounds (2.3 kg) pork shoulder, trimmed of fat and cut into 3-inch (7.5 cm) chunks
¼ cup (60 ml) beer
¾ teaspoon liquid smoke
8 hamburger buns or kaiser rolls

1. **To make the coleslaw (start 1 day ahead of serving):** In a large bowl with a lid or a resealable plastic bag, combine the cabbage and carrots.

2. In a medium bowl, whisk together the mayonnaise, sugar, milk, lemon juice, white vinegar, kosher salt, and black pepper. Add the mayonnaise mixture to the cabbage and carrots, close the container, and shake to combine. Refrigerate overnight.

3. **To make the pork rub:** In a small container with a lid, add all the rub ingredients, cover the container, and shake to combine. Set aside.

(continued on next page)

4. **To make the mop sauce:** In a food processor, combine the apple and white vinegar. Process until blended and transfer to a 2-quart (1.9 L) saucepan over medium-low heat.

5. Add the remaining mop sauce ingredients to the saucepan and stir to combine. Let simmer for 15 minutes. Remove from the heat. Once cooled, pour sauce into a squirt bottle.

6. **To make the pulled pork:** In a large bowl, with clean hands, massage ½ cup (80 g) pork rub into the pork pieces.

7. On your pressure cooker, select Sauté or Browning and fully heat the cooking pot.

8. Add the seasoned pork to the cooking pot and sear for about 15 seconds per side.

9. Pour in ½ cup (120 ml) mop sauce, the beer, and liquid smoke, and combine with the pork. Deglaze the cooking pot, scraping up any browned bits from the bottom of the pot.

10. Lock the lid and close the pressure valve. Cook for 40 minutes on High Pressure. When the beep sounds, allow a full natural pressure release.

11. Open the lid and transfer the pork to a large bowl. Using 2 forks, shred the pork. Add 1 cup (240 ml) of cooking liquid, if needed.

12. Serve the pork on buns, topped with a scoop of coleslaw and a squirt of mop sauce.

Notes

_____

_____

_____

_____

_____

_____

_____

Orange-Glazed Pork Chops

PREP: 10 MIN.
COOK: 3 MIN.
YIELD: 4 SERVINGS

This dish is for super-busy people who just want to come home from work and have a delicious, hot meal in under 20 minutes (see TOG Tip!).

½ cup (120 ml) frozen orange juice concentrate
¼ cup (60 g) packed dark brown sugar
2 tablespoons (30 ml) soy sauce
1 tablespoon (15 ml) Worcestershire sauce
1 tablespoon (15 ml) freshly squeezed lemon juice
¼ cup (60 ml) brandy or bourbon
1 shallot, diced
3 garlic cloves, minced
½ teaspoon ground cinnamon
1 teaspoon Sambal Oelek Ground Fresh Chili Paste
2 pounds (907 g) bone-in pork chops (¾ inch, or 2 cm, thick), trimmed of fat
2 tablespoons (28 g) salted butter
Zest of 1 orange

1. In a medium bowl, add the orange juice concentrate, brown sugar, soy and Worcestershire sauces, lemon juice, brandy, shallot, garlic, cinnamon, and cayenne. Whisk to combine. Add the pork chops and marinate in the refrigerator overnight.

2. Add the pork chops and marinade to the pressure cooker cooking pot.

3. Lock the lid and close the pressure valve. Cook for 3 minutes on High Pressure. When the beep sounds, wait 10 minutes, then release any remaining pressure.

4. Remove the lid and stir the butter into the sauce. Simmer to thicken the sauce. Stir in the orange zest.

5. Serve the pork chops with the sauce spooned over the top.

💜 **TOG TIP!**
This is a great make-ahead freezer meal, as the pork chops need to marinate overnight.

Pork Carnitas
(Mexican Pulled Pork)

PREP: 20 MIN.
COOK: 40 MIN.
YIELD: 6–8 SERVINGS

These are seriously the best pork carnitas you will ever taste—crispy yet deliciously moist and full of deep, complex flavors. This dish is perfect for Cinco de Mayo parties, as the carnitas can be made in advance and fried right before serving.

2 tablespoons (30 ml) kosher salt

1 tablespoon (15 ml) ground cumin

2 teaspoons dried oregano

¼ teaspoon freshly ground black pepper

5 pounds (2.2 kg) boneless pork butt, trimmed, cut into pieces, and 3-inch (7.5 cm) piece of fat reserved

4 large oranges, divided

10 garlic cloves, minced

2 cinnamon sticks

2 bay leaves

1 large onion, chopped

1 large jalapeño pepper, stemmed, seeded, and chopped

2 limes, divided

2 tablespoons (30 ml) extra-virgin olive oil, plus more as needed

Fresh cilantro leaves, for garnishing

♥ TOG TIPS!

Serve with shredded cabbage, lime wedges, sliced avocado, and Pico de Gallo (page 12).

Top with a crumbling cheese, such as cotija, or even feta. (Feta has a similar taste to cotija.) A melting cheese, such as Oaxaca, mozzarella, or Monterey Jack, is great too.

1. In a large bowl, combine the kosher salt, cumin, oregano, and black pepper. Add the pork pieces and massage the rub into the pork.

2. On your pressure cooker, select Sauté or Browning and fully heat the cooking pot.

3. Add the reserved pork fat to the pot and sauté for 3 minutes to render.

4. Add the juice of 1 orange and deglaze the cooking pot, scraping up any browned bits from the bottom of the pot. Turn off the pressure cooker.

5. Place the seasoned pork into the cooking pot. Add the garlic, cinnamon sticks, bay leaves, onion, and jalapeño.

6. Squeeze the juice of the remaining 3 oranges and 1 lime into the pot.

7. Lock the lid and close the pressure valve. Cook for 40 minutes on High Pressure. When the beep sounds, allow a 20-minute (or full) natural pressure release.

8. Remove the lid and transfer the meat to a colander to drain the liquid. Place the drained pork into a large bowl and use 2 forks to shred it well.

9. On your pressure cooker, select Sauté or Browning and simmer the sauce for about 10 minutes to reduce liquid. Pour the liquid into a large heat-resistant cup and skim off the fat.

10. Heat a cast-iron skillet over medium-high heat for 10 minutes.

11. Add the olive oil to the skillet and some shredded pork. Wait 1 minute and add ½ cup (120 ml) of the hot carnitas liquid. Fry the pork on one side until the liquid evaporates. Transfer the carnitas to a serving platter. Repeat with the remaining meat and liquid until done. Drizzle a little carnitas liquid over the pork.

12. Squeeze the juice of the remaining lime over the pork and garnish with cilantro (see TOG Tips!).

Notes

Lechon Asado
(Cuban Garlic Pork with Mojo Sauce)

PREP: 2 H. 15 MIN.
COOK: 4 MIN.
YIELD: 4 SERVINGS

This popular Cuban pork dish in South Florida, made with lots of garlic and sour oranges, is best served with rice and black beans. The recipe can be made straight away; however, marinating the pork overnight is what makes this dish shine.

Mojo Sauce

1¼ cups freshly squeezed Seville orange juice (or ½ cup, or 120 ml, orange juice plus ¾ cup, or 180 ml, lime juice)
½ cup garlic, minced (about 2 or 3 heads)
3 tablespoons (45 ml) extra-virgin olive oil
1 tablespoon (15 ml) dried oregano
1 tablespoon (15 ml) kosher salt
2 teaspoons ground cumin
½ teaspoon freshly ground black pepper
¼ teaspoon red pepper flakes

Pork

4 to 5 pounds (1.8 to 2.2 kg) boneless pork shoulder (butt), trimmed and cut into 3-inch (7.5 cm) chunks
4 or 5 large onions, sliced ½ inch (13 mm) thick (do not break apart the slices)

1. **To make the mojo sauce:** In a large container or resealable plastic bag (large enough to hold the sauce and pork), combine all the mojo sauce ingredients.

2. **To make the pork:** Add the pork to the sauce, seal the container, and refrigerate for at least 2 hours or up to overnight.

3. Add the pork and marinade to the pressure cooker cooking pot. Place the onions on top of the pork.

4. Lock the lid and close the pressure valve. Cook for 4 minutes on High Pressure. When the beep sounds, allow a full natural pressure release.

5. Serve with Frijoles Negros (page 157) and rice (see TOG Tip!).

💜 **TOG TIP!**
Use the Perfectly Cooked Pot-in-Pot Rice recipe (page 153) and cook it at the same time as the lechon asado.

Balsamic-Spiced Apple Pork Tenderloin

PREP: 10 MIN.
COOK: 0 MIN.
YIELD: 6 SERVINGS

This pork tenderloin makes a beautiful presentation for a holiday dinner. The aroma of cloves and cinnamon lends a homey feeling to the kitchen.

Balsamic Reduction

½ cup (120 ml) balsamic vinegar
2 tablespoons (30 g) packed light brown sugar
⅛ teaspoon ground ginger
Pinch ground cloves

Rub

2 tablespoons (30 ml) grapeseed or extra-virgin olive oil
1 tablespoon (6 g) grated orange zest
2 teaspoons herbes de Provence
½ teaspoon sea salt
¼ teaspoon freshly ground black pepper

Pork

2 pork tenderloins, silverskin removed
1 tablespoon (15 ml) grapeseed or vegetable oil
½ cup (120 ml) apple cider
1 cinnamon stick
3 Granny Smith apples, peeled, cored, and quartered (see TOG Tip!)
2 tablespoons (28 g) salted butter

♥ TOG TIP!

Granny Smith apples hold up best under pressure; however, if they become mushy, smash them to make applesauce.

1. **To make the balsamic reduction:** In a small bowl, whisk together all the reduction ingredients. Set aside.

2. **To make the rub:** In a large bowl, whisk together all the rub ingredients.

3. **To make the pork:** Massage the rub into the pork.

4. On your pressure cooker, select Sauté or Browning and fully heat the cooking pot.

5. Add the grapeseed oil. Add the tenderloins to the cooking pot, one at a time, and sear well on all sides. Transfer the pork to a plate.

6. Pour in the apple cider and deglaze the cooking pot, scraping up any browned bits from the bottom of the pot.

7. Pour in half of the balsamic reduction and add the cinnamon stick. Simmer until reduced by half, or until syrupy. Turn off the pressure cooker.

8. Return the tenderloins to the cooking pot and place the apples on top.

9. Lock the lid and close the pressure valve. Cook for 0 minutes on Low Pressure. When the beep sounds, wait 5 minutes, then release the remaining pressure.

10. Remove the lid and transfer the pork and apples to a plate, cover with aluminum foil, and allow the juices to redistribute.

11. On your pressure cooker, select Sauté or Browning, whisk in the remaining balsamic reduction, and simmer the liquid for 5 minutes. Whisk in the butter to thicken the sauce and serve it over the pork.

Okinawan Shoyu Pork

PREP: 15 MIN.
COOK: 20 MIN.
YIELD: 4 SERVINGS

Popular in Hawaii, this pork dish is braised and cooked in a sweet, salty, and fragrant marinade.

2 tablespoons (30 ml) cooking oil

2 pounds (907 g) pork belly, sliced 2 inches (5 cm) thick

½ cup (120 ml) chicken broth

½ cup (120 ml) sake

½ cup (120 ml) shoyu (Japanese soy sauce)

¼ cup (60 ml) mirin

½ cup (100 g) packed light brown sugar

3-inch (7.5 cm) piece fresh ginger, unpeeled, sliced ¼ inch (6 mm) thick, and smashed

2 garlic cloves, peeled and smashed

Cooked rice, for serving

4 scallions, chopped, for garnishing

1. On your pressure cooker, select Sauté or Browning and fully heat the cooking pot.

2. Add the oil and pork belly to the cooking pot. Brown the pork well on all sides and transfer to a plate.

3. Pour out any excess oil from the cooking pot.

4. Pour in the chicken broth and deglaze the cooking pot, scraping up any browned bits from the bottom of the pot.

5. Add the sake, shoyu, mirin, brown sugar, ginger, and garlic.

6. Return the pork belly to the cooking pot.

7. Lock the lid and close the pressure valve. Cook for 20 minutes on High Pressure. When the beep sounds, wait 15 minutes, then release the remaining pressure.

8. Serve the pork over the rice, spoon on a little sauce, and garnish with the chopped scallions (see TOG Tip!).

♥ **TOG TIP!**

Serve with pickled ginger and/or pickled daikon. The acidity of the pickled ginger or daikon will balance out the sweetness of the sauce.

Pork Chops in Homemade Mushroom Gravy

PREP: 10 MIN.
COOK: 6 MIN.
YIELD: 2–4 SERVINGS

Moist, tender, and full of flavor, the bone-in pork chops cook in my delicious, homemade gravy.

Gravy

1 cup (240 ml) cold milk
1 tablespoon (15 ml) potato starch
2 tablespoons (28 g) salted butter
½ teaspoon sea salt
¼ teaspoon freshly ground black pepper

Pork Chops

4 bone-in, ½-inch-thick (13 mm) pork chops (see TOG Tips!)
1 tablespoon (15 ml) TOG House Seasoning (page 10)
2 tablespoons (30 ml) potato starch
2 tablespoons (30 ml) extra-virgin olive oil
8 ounces (227 g) cremini mushrooms, sliced
½ cup (80 g) onion, sliced
2 garlic cloves, minced
¼ cup (60 ml) dry sherry
1¼ cups (300 ml) chicken stock or broth

💜 **TOG TIPS!**

For thicker pork chops, add 1 minute to the cooking time.

Add a trivet and a pan of diced potatoes above the pork to make mashed potatoes for a pot-in-pot meail.

1. **To make the gravy:** In a small bowl, whisk together all the gravy ingredients. Set aside.

2. **To make the pork chops:** Pat the chops dry with a paper towel and season both sides well with the house seasoning. Dredge the pork chops through the potato starch.

3. On your pressure cooker, select Sauté or Browning and fully heat the cooking pot.

4. Add the olive oil to the cooking pot. One at a time, sear each chop for about 5 seconds per side. Transfer to a plate.

5. Add the mushrooms and onion. Sauté for 3 minutes.

6. Add the garlic. Sauté for 1 minute more, being careful not to let the garlic burn.

7. Pour in the sherry and deglaze the cooking pot, scraping up any browned bits from the bottom of the pot.

8. Add the chicken broth and gravy to the cooking pot. Stir until the butter (in the gravy) melts.

9. Add the pork chops and any accumulated juices back into the cooking pot and submerge in the gravy.

10. Lock the lid and close the pressure valve. Cook for 6 minutes on High Pressure. When the beep sounds, wait 10 minutes, then release the remaining pressure.

11. Remove the lid and transfer the pork chops to a serving plate.

12. Select Sauté or Browning on the pressure cooker. Simmer to thicken the gravy.

Vietnamese-Style Meatballs in Sauce

PREP: 25 MIN.
COOK: 10 MIN.
YIELD: 4 SERVINGS

My Vietnamese meatballs can be enjoyed on their own with *nuoc cham*, in a hot bowl of pho, or cooked in my simple tomato sauce. Serve with rice or rice noodles.

Meatballs

⅓ cup (55 g) onion
⅓ cup (45 g) jicama
2 scallions
1½ tablespoons (23 ml) fish sauce
2 tablespoons (30 ml) potato starch
1 tablespoon (15 ml) extra-virgin olive oil
½ teaspoon freshly ground black pepper
1 pound (454 g) ground pork

Sauce

1 tablespoon (15 ml) extra-virgin olive oil
¼ cup (40 g) onion, finely minced
2 garlic cloves, minced
1 can (15 ounces, or 425 g) diced tomatoes
1 can (15 ounces, or 425 g) crushed
  tomatoes
2 tablespoons (30 ml) sugar
1 tablespoon (15 ml) salt
1 tablespoon (15 ml) fish sauce
Fresh cilantro leaves, for garnishing

1. **To make the meatballs:** In a food processor, combine the onion, jicama, scallions, fish sauce, potato starch, olive oil, and black pepper. Process until smooth.

2. Add the pork and pulse until combined, pausing to scrape down the sides of the bowl as needed (see TOG Tip!). Form the mixture into 20 meatballs and set aside.

3. **To make the sauce:** Add all the sauce ingredients to the pressure cooker cooking pot.

4. Carefully place the meatballs in the sauce.

5. Lock the lid and close the pressure valve. Cook for 10 minutes on Low Pressure. When the beep sounds, wait 10 minutes, then release the remaining pressure.

6. Serve garnished with cilantro.

♥ **TOG TIP!**

Did you know that processing the ingredients for meatballs in a food processor produces a tighter meatball? Plus, no chopping!

MEAT-LOVER FAMILY FAVORITES

FRENCH DIP • *Pot Roast*

SLOPPY JOES • DRIVE-THRU TACOS

CABBAGE AND SAUSAGE

TURKEY MEATLOAF

BARBECUE MEATBALLS

Salisbury Steak GYROS

BEEF STROGANOFF

SPICED LAMB SHANKS GREEK

BRAISED SHORT RIBS MEATBALLS

AND *Cali-mex stuffed Peppers*

French Dip Sandwiches

PREP: 15 MIN.
COOK: 55 MIN.
YIELD: 6–8 SERVINGS

An American sandwich creation, the "French" dip was probably given its name because the French bread fell into the au jus.

1 chuck roast (3 to 4 pounds, or 1.3 to 1.8 kg), trimmed of fat and quartered
1 large onion, diced
1 medium carrot, minced
1¼ cups (10 ounces, or 300 ml) beef consommé or broth
¼ cup (60 ml) red wine vinegar
3 garlic cloves, minced
1 jar (16 ounces, or 454 g) pepperoncini, divided, plus more for topping sandwiches
1 tablespoon (15 ml) dried oregano
2 teaspoons kosher salt
1½ teaspoons dried parsley
½ teaspoon freshly ground black pepper
½ teaspoon dried basil
⅛ teaspoon dried thyme
⅛ teaspoon celery seed
Butter at room temperature
6 to 8 French bread rolls, sliced in half
Garlic powder, to taste
Melting cheese (such as mozzarella, Monterey Jack, or Oaxaca)

1. In the pressure cooker cooking pot, combine the beef, onion, carrot, beef consommé, red wine vinegar, garlic, half the juice from the pepperoncini jar, 16 pepperoncini peppers, and the remaining seasonings.

2. Lock the lid and close the pressure valve. Cook for 45 minutes on High Pressure. When the beep sounds, allow a full natural pressure release.

3. Remove the meat from the pot and thinly slice it or shred it.

4. Skim the fat from the cooking liquid (see TOG Tip!).

5. Butter both sides of the rolls and lightly sprinkle with garlic powder. Place under the broiler, cut side up, and lightly brown.

6. Add the meat to the bottom buns and cover with cheese. Broil a few seconds, or until melted. Remove from the oven and top with pepperoncinis. Dip the cut sides of the top buns quickly into the au jus and place on top of the sandwiches.

7. Serve with small bowls of au jus for dipping.

💜 **TOG TIP!**
You can cook the meat the day before and refrigerate it and the au jus. Peel off the layer of fat that solidifies and reheat the juice with the meat.

Sunday Night Pot Roast

Make Sunday night a family and friends night with this pot roast and a bottle of dry Bordeaux.

PREP: 25 MIN.
COOK: 38 MIN.
YIELD: 6 SERVINGS

1 chuck roast (4 to 5 pounds, or 1.8 to 2.2 kg)

1 tablespoon (15 ml) kosher salt, or to taste

2 teaspoons freshly ground black pepper

2 tablespoons (30 ml) extra-virgin olive oil, plus more as needed

3 medium onions, peeled and halved

4 large carrots, unpeeled and cut in half

½ cup (120 ml) dry red wine

8 ounces (227 g) cremini mushrooms, cleaned and halved

4 garlic cloves, minced

1 tablespoon (15 ml) fish sauce

1 tablespoon (15 ml) Worcestershire sauce

3 fresh rosemary sprigs

3 fresh thyme sprigs

2 bay leaves

¾ cup (180 ml) beef broth

5 medium Yukon Gold potatoes, cut in half

💟 **TOG TIP!**

If you would like gravy, make a slurry by transferring ½ cup (120 ml) liquid from the cooking pot to a small bowl and whisking in 2 tablespoons (23 g) potato starch. Remove and discard the bay leaves from the cooking pot and slowly whisk in the slurry. Season the gravy to taste with salt and pepper.

1. Trim the fat and cut out the connective tissue from the roast. Season the roast with the kosher salt and black pepper.

2. On your pressure cooker, select Sauté or Browning and fully heat the cooking pot.

3. Add the olive oil and onion halves, cut side down, to the cooking pot. Let sit undisturbed for 3 minutes. Turn each half over and sear for 3 minutes more, or until both sides are browned. Transfer the onions to a plate. Add the carrots and sear to brown, about 3 minutes. Transfer the carrots to the plate with the onions.

4. Place the roast into pot and sear for about 30 seconds per side, until browned. Transfer the roast to a plate.

5. Pour in the red wine and deglaze the cooking pot, scraping up any browned bits from the bottom of the pot.

6. Add the mushrooms and garlic to the cooking pot. Place the roast on top of the mushrooms. Add the fish sauce, Worcestershire sauce, rosemary, thyme, and bay leaves. Pour in the beef broth.

7. Lock the lid and close the pressure valve. Cook for 35 minutes on High Pressure. When the beep sounds, wait 10 minutes, then release any remaining pressure.

8. Remove the lid and add the potatoes, carrots, and onions. Lock the lid and close the pressure valve. Cook for 3 minutes on High Pressure. When the beep sounds, wait 10 minutes, then release any remaining pressure.

9. Transfer the roast and vegetables to a serving platter (see TOG Tip!). Remove and discard the bay leaves.

Sloppy Joes

Take a trip back to your childhood with this all-American, homemade sloppy Joe recipe.

PREP: 25 MIN.
COOK: 3 MIN.
YIELD: 4 SERVINGS

1 tablespoon (15 ml) extra-virgin olive oil
1¼ cups (200 g) onion, diced
1¼ cups (200 g) green bell pepper, diced
2 garlic cloves, finely minced
1½ pounds (680 g) lean ground beef
¼ cup (60 ml) red wine vinegar
2½ tablespoons (38 ml) Worcestershire sauce
3½ tablespoons (53 g) packed dark brown sugar
1½ cups (12 ounces, or 375 g) tomato puree (see TOG Tip!)
2 teaspoons sea salt
½ teaspoon freshly ground black pepper
1 teaspoon chili powder
½ teaspoon dry mustard
¼ teaspoon red pepper flakes
¼ cup (60 ml) water
2 tablespoons (32 g) tomato paste
8 large hamburger buns, buttered and lightly toasted

1. On your pressure cooker, select Sauté or Browning and fully heat the cooking pot.

2. Add the olive oil and coat the bottom of the cooking pot.

3. Add the onion, green bell pepper, garlic, and ground beef. Sauté until the beef is slightly browned. Use a splatter guard and carefully pour out the grease.

4. Pour in the red wine vinegar and deglaze the cooking pot, scraping up any browned bits from the bottom of the pot.

5. Stir in the Worcestershire sauce, brown sugar, and tomato puree. Add the sea salt, black pepper, chili powder, dry mustard, red pepper flakes, water, and tomato paste. Combine well.

6. Lock the lid and close the pressure valve. Cook for 3 minutes on High Pressure. When the beep sounds, wait 10 minutes, then release the remaining pressure.

7. Remove the lid and select Sauté or Browning. Simmer until much of the liquid evaporates and the consistency is thick.

8. Serve on the toasted hamburger buns.

♥ **TOG TIP!**

A good quality tomato puree, such as San Marzano brand from Italy, will yield better results than an inexpensive brand. Tomato puree is thicker and more flavorful than tomato sauce, so be sure to use the puree.

Drive-Thru Tacos

Enjoy fresh, hot, homemade tacos right in your own home, without wondering what lurks in the meat.

PREP: 15 MIN.
COOK: 3 MIN.
YIELD: 4 SERVINGS

Seasoning Mix

1 tablespoon (15 ml) mild chili powder
¼ teaspoon garlic powder
¼ teaspoon onion powder
¼ teaspoon dried minced onion
1½ teaspoons ground cumin
¼ teaspoon dried oregano
½ teaspoon paprika
Pinch cayenne pepper
¾ teaspoon sea salt
½ teaspoon freshly ground black pepper

Meat

1 tablespoon (15 ml) extra-virgin olive oil
1 pound (454 g) ground beef or turkey
1¼ cups (300 ml) beef broth, divided
1 tablespoon (15 ml) Worcestershire
   sauce
2 teaspoons masa (corn flour)

Serving

12 taco shells
Shredded lettuce
Diced tomatoes
Shredded cheese
Sour cream or plain yogurt
Hot sauce

1. **To make the seasoning mix:** In a small bowl, combine all the seasoning mix ingredients. Set aside.

2. **To make the meat:** On your pressure cooker, select Sauté or Browning and fully heat the cooking pot.

3. Add the olive oil, ground beef, and ½ cup (120 ml) of the beef broth to the pot. Use a fork or masher and break apart the meat. Sauté until the meat is browned, about 3 minutes. The meat should be completely mashed and crumbled.

4. Turn off the pressure cooker and pour out any excess liquid. Scrape up any browned bits from the bottom of the pot.

5. Stir in the seasoning mix, Worcestershire sauce, and remaining ¾ cup (180 ml) beef broth.

6. Lock the lid and close the pressure valve. Cook for 3 minutes on High Pressure. When the beep sounds, wait 10 minutes, then release any remaining pressure.

7. Remove the lid and sprinkle the masa over the meat mixture. Stir, while simmering, until the liquid evaporates.

8. Serve in taco shells with toppings as desired.

Turkey Meatloaf and Mashed Potatoes

PREP: 15 MIN.
COOK: 20 MIN.
YIELD: 4 SERVINGS

Truly an American comfort meal. Sometimes the simplest things in life are the best, and this easy recipe will have you feeling warm all over.

4 large white or Yukon Gold potatoes, peeled (left whole; see TOG Tips!)

1½ pounds (680 g) ground turkey (you can substitute ground beef)

¾ cup (120 g) onion, finely diced

¾ cup (87 g) Grape-Nuts cereal

¼ cup (12 g) panko bread crumbs

2 tablespoons (30 ml) Worcestershire sauce

1 large egg

1 teaspoon kosher salt, or to taste

1 teaspoon onion powder

1 teaspoon garlic powder

1 can (15 ounces, or 425 g) diced tomatoes, drained

2 cups (480 ml) water, for the cooking pot

2 tablespoons (30 ml) sugar

💜 **TOG TIPS!**

Do not cut up the potatoes. Because of the longer cook time, they need to remain whole to prevent overcooked, waterlogged potatoes.

For a different spin on mashed potatoes, try Buffy's Carrot Mash (page 166).

1. Place the peeled potatoes in a bowl of cool water and set aside.

2. In a large bowl, combine the turkey, onion, cereal, panko, Worcestershire sauce, egg, salt, onion powder, and garlic powder.

3. Place the diced tomatoes in a medium bowl and use an immersion blender to blend them. Add half of the pulverized tomatoes to the meat mixture and combine. Reserve the remaining pulverized tomatoes.

4. Form the meat mixture into a tall, oval loaf shape and place it on a steamer rack.

5. Place a short-legged stainless-steel trivet into the cooking pot and add the water to the pot. Lay the whole potatoes in a single row on top of the trivet. Place the steamer rack with the meatloaf on top of the potatoes.

6. Lock the lid and close the pressure valve. Cook for 20 minutes on High Pressure. When the beep sounds, wait 10 minutes, then release the remaining pressure.

7. Preheat the oven broiler.

8. Add the sugar to the reserved pulverized tomatoes and mix well.

9. Remove the lid and transfer the meatloaf to an oven-safe dish. Pour three-fourths of the reserved pulverized tomatoes on top of the meatloaf and place under the broiler for 5 minutes.

10. While the meatloaf is in the oven, mash the potatoes in the cooking pot (see Mashed Potatoes, page 13).

11. Serve the meatloaf with the mashed potatoes and the remaining sauce spooned over the top.

Barbecue Meatballs

These meatballs are delicious as a main course, served with a side of Buffy's Carrot Mash (page 166), or they can be used for making meatball subs.

PREP: 25 MIN.
COOK: 10 MIN.
YIELD: 12 MEATBALLS

Barbecue Sauce

¾ cup (188 g) tomato puree
⅓ cup (75 g) packed dark brown sugar
¼ cup (40 g) onion, finely diced
1 garlic clove, minced
¼ cup (60 ml) red wine vinegar
¼ cup (60 ml) water
1½ teaspoons liquid smoke
1 teaspoon kosher salt, plus more as needed
½ teaspoon freshly ground black pepper, plus more as needed
½ teaspoon Worcestershire sauces

Meatballs

1½ pounds (680 g) lean ground beef or turkey
1 cup (95 g) old-fashioned rolled oats (not instant)
1 small onion, minced
1 large egg
½ cup (120 ml) evaporated milk
1 tablespoon (15 ml) Worcestershire sauce
1 teaspoon extra-virgin olive oil
1 teaspoon garlic powder
1 teaspoon freshly ground black pepper, plus more as needed
1 teaspoon kosher salt, plus more as needed
¾ teaspoon chili powder

1. **To make the barbecue sauce:** In your pressure cooker cooking pot, combine all the sauce ingredients.

2. **To make the meatballs:** In a large bowl, combine all the meatball ingredients (see TOG Tips!). Form the mixture into 12 meatballs.

3. Add the meatballs to the sauce in the cooking pot.

4. Lock the lid and close the pressure valve. Cook for 10 minutes on Low Pressure. When the beep sounds, allow a full natural pressure release.

5. Remove the lid and transfer the meatballs to a serving bowl. On your pressure cooker, select Sauté or Browning, and simmer, stirring constantly, until the sauce thickens. Taste and season with more salt and black pepper, as needed.

6. Pour the sauce over the meatballs and serve.

💜 **TOG TIPS!**

The meatballs can be mixed in a food processor, if you prefer. Add all ingredients except for the ground meat and process. Then add the meat and pulse to combine.

The meatballs can be browned in extra-virgin olive oil in a skillet on the stove first, if desired.

Salisbury Steak

This is not your TV dinner Salisbury steak. Don't set up a TV tray in front of your couch or recliner; clear the table and enjoy. Make it a pot-in-pot meal with mashed potatoes (page 13).

PREP: 20 MIN.
COOK: 4 MIN.
YIELD: 4–6 SERVINGS

Gravy

2½ cups (600 ml) water
1 tablespoon (17 g) beef base
1 tablespoon (15 g) Dijon mustard
1 tablespoon (15 ml) Worcestershire sauce
1 tablespoon (15 ml) soy sauce
1 tablespoon (15 ml) potato starch
1 teaspoon kosher salt
½ teaspoon freshly ground black pepper

Steaks

¼ cup (40 g) onion, diced, plus 1 large onion, thickly sliced, divided
2 garlic cloves
1 tablespoon (15 ml) Worcestershire sauce
1 tablespoon (15 ml) soy sauce
1 tablespoon tomato paste
½ teaspoon beef base (see TOG Tips!)
1 large egg
½ cup (48 g) old-fashioned rolled oats (not instant)
½ teaspoon dry mustard
¼ teaspoon freshly ground black pepper
¼ teaspoon paprika
1 pound (454 g) ground beef
2 tablespoons (30 ml) potato starch
1 teaspoon extra-virgin olive oil
4 tablespoons (56 g) salted butter, divided
8 ounces (227 g) cremini mushrooms, sliced
¼ cup (60 ml) red wine

1. **To make the gravy:** Whisk together all the gravy ingredients. Set aside.

2. **To make the steaks:** In a food processor, add ¼ cup (40 g) of the onion, the garlic, Worcestershire sauce, soy sauce, tomato paste, beef base, egg, oats, dry mustard, pepper, and paprika. Process until well chopped, then add the ground beef and pulse until well combined (see TOG Tips!).

3. Shape the beef mixture into 6 oval, flat steaks.

4. Place the potato starch in a shallow bowl and dredge the steaks through the potato starch.

5. On your pressure cooker, select Sauté or Browning and preheat the cooking pot fully.

6. Add the oil to the cooking pot and swirl to coat the bottom, then add 2 tablespoons (28 g) of the butter.

7. Working in batches, sear the steaks on both sides for 10 seconds and remove to a plate.

8. Add the remaining 2 tablespoons (28 g) butter, the mushrooms, and half of the sliced onion. Sauté for 3 minutes.

9. Add the red wine and deglaze the cooking pot, scraping up any browned bits from the bottom of the pot.

10. Add the gravy to the pot and combine. Carefully place the steaks into the cooking pot and cover with the remaining half of sliced onion.

11. Lock the lid and close the pressure valve. Cook for 4 minutes on High Pressure. When the beep sounds, wait 10 minutes, then release the remaining pressure.

12. Remove the steaks. Turn off the pressure cooker.

13. Select Sauté or Browning and simmer the gravy to thicken to desired consistency.

♥ **TOG TIPS!**

Better Than Bouillon Beef Base is my choice for the best "flavor bomb". It gives the steaks an intense beef flavor.

Processing the steak ingredients in a food processor helps the patties stay together nicely—more like a steak than a hamburger. If you don't have a food processor, mince the onion and garlic as finely as possible.

Notes

_____

_____

_____

_____

_____

_____

_____

_____

_____

_____

Beef and Lamb Gyros

Delicious street food, these gyros will make you feel like you are vacationing on a Greek island.

PREP: 20 MIN.
COOK: 20 MIN.
YIELD: 4–6 SERVINGS

Gyros

1 small onion
8 garlic cloves
2 teaspoons ground marjoram
2 teaspoons dried rosemary
2 teaspoons dried oregano
2 teaspoons kosher salt
¼ teaspoon freshly ground black pepper
2 pounds (907 g) ground lamb or beef, or a combination (see TOG Tips!)
1½ cups (360 ml) water, for the cooking pot

Serving

4 Greek pita breads
Tzatziki Sauce (page 11; see TOG Tips!)
Feta cheese
Chopped tomatoes
Thinly sliced onions
Shredded lettuce
Thinly sliced cucumber

1. In a food processor, chop the onion well. Transfer to a paper towel and squeeze out all the liquid. Return the onion to the processor and add the garlic, marjoram, rosemary, oregano, kosher salt, and black pepper. Process until the garlic is minced.

2. Add the meat and process until well combined. Transfer the meat mixture to a 6-inch (15 cm) loaf pan, pressing it in until it is very tight and compact. Cover the pan with aluminum foil and use a sharp knife to slice a vent hole in the center.

3. Place a short-legged stainless-steel trivet into the pressure cooker cooking pot and add the water to the pot. Place the loaf pan on the trivet.

4. Lock the lid and close the pressure valve. Cook for 20 minutes on High Pressure. When the beep sounds, wait 10 minutes, then release the remaining pressure.

5. Remove the lid and take the loaf pan out of the pressure cooker. Let rest for 15 minutes. Remove the gyro meat from the pan and thinly slice. Crisp the meat under the broiler or in an air fryer, if desired.

6. Serve in pita breads with tzatziki sauce and toppings as desired.

💜 **TOG TIPS!**

Gyros can be made with just beef or just lamb, or any combination of ground turkey, beef, lamb, bison, etc.

For maximum flavor, prepare the tzatziki sauce in advance, at least an hour or up to overnight

Greek Meatballs

PREP: 25 MIN.
COOK: 4 MIN.
YIELD: 4–6 SERVINGS

The aroma of cinnamon, mint, and cumin from these Greek meatballs (*keftedes*) will have your mouth watering and your tummy growling.

- ¾ cup (71 g) old-fashioned rolled oats (not instatnt)
- 4 ounces (113 g) red onion, peeled and quartered
- 1 large egg
- 4 tablespoons (60 ml) extra-virgin olive oil, divided
- 3 teaspoons (3 g) fresh mint leaves
- 1 teaspoon kosher salt
- ½ teaspoon ground cumin
- ½ teaspoon dried oregano
- ¼ teaspoon ground cinnamon
- ¼ teaspoon freshly ground black pepper
- 1 pound (454 g) lean ground beef or lamb
- 8 ounces (227 g) ground pork
- ¼ cup (60 ml) distilled white vinegar
- Lemon zest, for garnishing
- ½ lemon, for garnishing
- Cubed feta cheese, for serving
- 1 cup (230 g) Tzatziki Sauce (page 11; see TOG Tips!), for serving

1. In a food processor, combine the oats, red onion, egg, 1 tablespoon (15 ml) of the olive oil, mint, kosher salt, cumin, oregano, cinnamon, and black pepper. Process until well chopped.

2. Add the beef and pork, and pulse to combine.

3. Add the remaining 3 tablespoons (45 ml) olive oil to the pressure cooker cooking pot.

4. Using 1½-tablespoon (23 ml) portions (see TOG Tips!), roll the meat mixture into small meatballs and place them in the cooking pot as you go. (I get 38 meatballs from this recipe.)

5. Pour the vinegar over the meatballs.

6. Lock the lid and close the pressure valve. Cook for 4 minutes on High Pressure. When the beep sounds, wait 10 minutes, then release any remaining pressure.

7. Garnish with lemon zest and a squeeze of lemon juice. Serve with feta cheese and tzatziki sauce.

♥ **TOG TIPS!**

For maximum flavor, prepare the tzatziki sauce in advance, at least an hour or up to overnight.

I use a 1½-tablespoon cookie scoop to quickly measure the meat mixture and then tightly roll into a ball.

Cabbage and Sausage

This lean, healthy, and hearty meal will be on your table in less than 30 minutes.

PREP: 5 MIN.
COOK: 1 MIN.
YIELD: 4 SERVINGS

1 pound (454 g) bratwurst or knockwurst (see TOG Tip!)

3 tablespoons salted butter (42 g), coconut oil (45 ml), or bacon fat (45 ml)

1 small head green cabbage, chopped

½ cup (80 g) onion, chopped

1 can (15 ounces, or 425 g) diced tomatoes

¼ teaspoon garlic salt

2 teaspoons ground turmeric

Salt, to taste

Freshly ground black pepper, to taste

1. On your pressure cooker, select Sauté or Browning and fully heat the cooking pot.

2. Add the sausage to the cooking pot and sear for 1 minute, turning, to brown lightly. Remove the grease and drain the sausage on a paper towel, if necessary.

3. Add the butter, cabbage, onion, tomatoes and their juice, garlic salt, and turmeric.

4. Lock the lid and close the pressure valve. Cook for 1 minute on High Pressure. When the beep sounds, wait 5 minutes, then release the remaining pressure.

5. Remove the lid and, if there is excess liquid, let it cook down until most of liquid has been reduced.

6. Season to taste with salt and pepper.

♥ **TOG TIP!**
Flavored sausage, such as chicken apple or turkey basil, is delicious in this recipe.

Cali-Mex Stuffed Peppers

PREP: 20 MIN.
COOK: 5 MIN.
YIELD: 4 SERVINGS

These beautiful and colorful peppers are stuffed with the flavors of the West. Check the TOG Tip! for a low-carb option.

Stuffed Peppers

4 large bell peppers, any color
½ medium onion, peeled and quartered
4 garlic cloves, peeled
1 or 2 jalapeño peppers, stemmed and seeded
¼ cup (15 g) fresh cilantro leaves
2 tablespoons (32 g) tomato paste
1 tablespoon (15 ml) chili powder
1 tablespoon (15 ml) masa (corn flour)
2 teaspoons kosher salt
1½ teaspoons ground cumin
½ teaspoon freshly ground black pepper
1 pound (454 g) very lean ground beef
4 ounces (115 g) frozen corn, thawed and drained
3 ounces (85 g) Monterey Jack cheese with jalapeños, shredded
3 ounces (85 g) black olives, sliced
1¼ cups (10 ounces, or 300 ml) enchilada sauce

Toppings

1 cup (115 g) Monterey Jack cheese with jalapeños, shredded
½ cup (115 g) sour cream
½ cup (30 g) fresh cilantro leaves, chopped

1. **To make the stuffed peppers:** Slice off the tops of the bell peppers and remove the ribs and seeds. Poke a small hole in the bottom of each bell pepper. Remove and discard the stems from the tops. Reserve the tops.

2. In a food processor, combine the reserved pepper tops, onion, garlic, jalapeño(s), cilantro, tomato paste, chili powder, masa, salt, cumin, and black pepper. Pulse until chunky, but not mushy.

3. Remove the blade and add the ground beef, corn, Jack cheese, and olives to the bowl. Combine well.

4. Place a stainless steel trivet into the pressure cooker cooking pot.

5. Stuff the peppers with the meat mixture and place them on top of the trivet. Pour the enchilada sauce over the stuffed peppers.

6. Lock the lid and close the pressure valve. Cook for 5 minutes on High Pressure. When the beep sounds, wait 10 minutes, then release any remaining pressure.

7. **To top the peppers:** Remove the lid and sprinkle the Jack cheese over each pepper. Lightly replace the lid and let sit until the cheese melts.

8. Plate the peppers and top with the sour cream and cilantro. Spoon enchilada sauce from the pot over the top.

♥ **TOG TIP!**

If following a low-carb diet, leave out the corn, beans, and masa, and add another ounce (28 g) of cheese.

Beef Stroganoff

Potato starch is used in place of flour in the rich and flavorful sauce, making this recipe gluten-free. Enjoy with wide egg noodles or low-carb noodles for a low-carb, gluten-free meal.

PREP: 20 MIN.
COOK: 3 MIN.
YIELD: 6 SERVINGS

2 pounds (907 g) sirloin steak, sliced across the grain into 2-inch (5 cm) strips

2 teaspoons kosher salt, plus more as needed

¾ teaspoon freshly ground black pepper, plus more as needed

¾ teaspoon Hungarian paprika

6 tablespoons (68 g) potato starch

2 teaspoons extra-virgin olive oil

3 tablespoons (42 g) salted butter, divided

½ cup (120 ml) dry sherry or Shaoxing wine, divided

1 pound (454 g) cremini or wild mushrooms, sliced

8 ounces (227 g) onion, sliced

3 garlic cloves, minced

1½ tablespoons (21 ml) Worcestershire sauce

1 tablespoon (15 ml) fish sauce

1½ tablespoons (21 g) Dijon mustard

1¼ cups (300 ml) low-sodium beef broth

8 ounces (225 g) sour cream

16 ounces (454 g) egg noodles, prepared according to the package directions

Fresh parsley leaves, for garnishing

1. Place the beef strips in a medium-size bowl and sprinkle with the kosher salt, black pepper, and paprika. Add the potato starch and combine thoroughly.

2. On your pressure cooker, select Sauté or Browning and fully heat the cooking pot.

3. Add the olive oil, 1½ tablespoons (21 g) of the butter, and the beef to the cooking pot. Sear the beef for about 1 minute, until lightly browned. Transfer the beef to a bowl. Pour in ¼ cup (60 ml) of the sherry and deglaze the cooking pot, scraping up any browned bits from the bottom of the pot.

4. Add the remaining 1½ tablespoons (21 g) butter, along with the mushrooms and onion, and sauté for 3 minutes. Add the garlic and sauté for 30 seconds, scraping up any browned bits from the bottom of the pot. Add the remaining ¼ cup (60 ml) sherry, along with the Worcestershire sauce, fish sauce, Dijon mustard, and beef broth.

5. Return the beef to the cooking pot along with any accumulated juices on the plate.

6. Lock the lid and close the pressure valve. Cook for 3 minutes on High Pressure. When the beep sounds, wait 10 minutes, then release the remaining pressure.

7. Remove the lid, taste, and season with more salt and black pepper, as needed. (Make sure the broth is highly seasoned, as the sour cream will dilute the flavor.)

8. Place the sour cream in a large measuring cup and slowly add ½ cup (120 ml) of hot liquid from the cooking pot to temper. Whisk together well. Slowly add the sour cream mixture back into the cooking pot and stir to combine (see TOG Tip!).

9. Serve over egg noodles, garnished with parsley.

♥ **TOG TIP!**

For a thicker sauce, make a slurry by combining ½ cup (120 ml) hot cooking liquid with 2 tablespoons (30 ml) potato starch. Whisk well and incorporate the slurry into the cooking pot before adding the sour cream.

Spiced Lamb Shanks

Perfect for the holidays or anytime you want an easy yet delicious "fancy" meal. Enjoy with mashed potatoes.

1 cup (240 ml) freshly squeezed orange juice
⅓ cup (115 g) honey
3 garlic cloves, sliced
2-inch (5 cm) piece fresh ginger, peeled and minced
⅛ teaspoon ground allspice
Pinch ground cloves
¼ cup (45 g) potato starch
1 tablespoon (15 ml) kosher salt
¼ teaspoon freshly ground black pepper
4 lamb shanks (see TOG Tips!)
2 tablespoons (30 ml) extra-virgin olive oil
¼ cup (60 ml) red wine
6 ounces (170 g) fresh cranberries
1 medium onion, roughly chopped
1 cinnamon stick
Zest of 1 orange, for serving

1. In a small bowl, whisk together the orange juice, honey, garlic, ginger, allspice, and cloves. Set aside.

2. In a shallow bowl, combine the potato starch, kosher salt, and black pepper. Dredge the lamb shanks through the seasoned potato starch. Set aside on a plate.

3. On your pressure cooker, select Sauté or Browning and fully heat the cooking pot.

4. Add the olive oil and lamb shanks, one at a time, to the cooking pot. Sear on all sides, about 30 seconds. Transfer the shanks to a plate.

5. Pour in the red wine and deglaze the cooking pot, scraping up any browned bits from the bottom of the pot.

6. Stir in the cranberries and onions, and return the lamb shanks to the cooking pot. Add the cinnamon stick and pour the orange-juice mixture over the shanks.

7. Lock the lid and close the pressure valve. Cook for 40 minutes on High Pressure. When the beep sounds, allow a full natural pressure release. Remove the lid and transfer the lamb shanks to a plate.

8. On your pressure cooker, select Sauté or Browning and simmer the sauce to thicken (see TOG Tips!).

9. Plate the lamb shanks and spoon the sauce over them. Sprinkle with orange zest before serving.

💜 **TOG TIPS!**

This recipe also can be made with chuck roast or pork shoulder.

For a thick, jellied sauce, remove the cinnamon stick and use an immersion blender to blend the sauce.

Red Wine-Braised Short Ribs

PREP: 30 MIN.
COOK: 45 MIN.
YIELD: 4 SERVINGS

These melt-in-your-mouth short ribs swim in a rich red wine sauce. This is a decadent meal and perfect for when you have company over for dinner. Serve with Creamy Goat Cheese Polenta (page 167).

8 beef bone-in short ribs, fat trimmed from the top

1 teaspoon kosher salt, plus more to taste

½ teaspoon freshly ground black pepper, plus more to taste

¼ cup (45 g) potato starch

2 tablespoons (30 ml) extra-virgin olive oil

3 ounces (85 g) pancetta, diced (see TOG Tip!)

1½ cups (360 ml) dry red wine

1½ cups (360 ml) beef broth

3 medium-size carrots, roughly chopped

2 medium-size shallots, roughly chopped

1 medium-size onion, chopped

2 fresh rosemary sprigs

2 fresh thyme sprigs

1. On your pressure cooker, select Sauté or Browning and fully heat the cooking pot.

2. Season the short ribs on all sides with the kosher salt and black pepper.

3. Place the potato starch in a shallow bowl and dredge the ribs through it. Shake off any excess starch and set aside.

4. Add the olive oil and pancetta to the cooking pot. Let bubble for 30 seconds. Add the ribs, 2 at a time, and sear for 15 seconds per side to brown. Transfer to a plate.

5. Pour in the red wine and beef broth, and deglaze the cooking pot, scraping up any browned bits from the bottom of the pot. Add the carrots, shallots, and onion to the cooking pot, and stir to combine. Turn off the pressure cooker.

6. Season with additional salt and pepper to taste, and return the ribs to the pot with any accumulated juices. Add the rosemary and thyme.

7. Lock the lid and close the pressure valve. Cook for 45 minutes on High Pressure. When the beep sounds, allow a full natural pressure release. Remove the lid.

8. Let the pot sit for 15 minutes. Carefully skim off the fat. Alternatively, place the cooking pot in the refrigerator for a few hours, or overnight. The fat will rise to the top and solidify, making it easier to remove. Short ribs taste even better the next day.

💛 **TOG TIP!**

If you keep kosher, do not eat pork or turkey bacon makes a good substitute for the pancetta.

EASY BOWLS

PAD THAI • VIETNAMESE BOWL

PAD SEE EW

EGG ROLL IN A BOWL

CHICKEN TACO BOWL

AND BLACK BEAN BOWL

Pad Thai Bowl

There are two things I order at Thai restaurants: green curry with tofu and mixed pad Thai. Pad Thai is easy to make yourself. For this recipe, just choose the protein(s) you like in any combination.

PREP: 20 MIN.
COOK: 1 MIN.
YIELD: 4 SERVINGS

Pad Thai

8 ounces (227 g) wide Thai rice noodles

¼ cup (60 ml) peanut, grapeseed, or vegetable oil

3 scallions, green tops separated from white roots, sliced ½ inch (13 mm) thick

4 ounces (113 g) extra-firm tofu, cut into 1½-inch (4 cm) strips

12 ounces (340 g) chicken, pork, or beef, or a combination, cut into 2-inch (5 cm) strips

1½ teaspoons minced garlic

2 large eggs

1½ cups (12 ounces, or 360 ml) chicken broth

8 large shrimp, cleaned, and tails on

Pad Thai Sauce

⅓ cup (65 g) packed light brown sugar

3 tablespoons (42 g) tamarind paste

2 tablespoons (30 ml) fish sauce

1 tablespoon (15 ml) freshly squeezed lime juice

1 teaspoon Sambal Oelek Ground Fresh Chili Paste

1 tablespoon (16 g) tomato paste

Garnish

1 medium carrot, shaved into ribbons

1 cup (50 g) bean sprouts

½ cup (30 g) fresh cilantro leaves, chopped

½ cup (75 g) unsalted roasted peanuts, crushed

1 lime, quartered

1. **To make the pad Thai:** In a large bowl, combine the rice noodles with enough hot water to cover and soak for 1 to 2 minutes, or until slightly bendable. Drain. Set aside.

2. **To make the pad Thai sauce:** In a large measuring cup or small bowl, whisk together the pad Thai sauce ingredients.

3. On your pressure cooker, select Sauté or Browning and fully heat the cooking pot.

4. Add the oil, sliced scallion root ends, and tofu to the cooking pot. Sauté for 1 minute. Add the meat and garlic. Sauté for 1 minute more.

5. Push everything to one side of the pot and crack the eggs into the empty side of the pot. Scramble them until almost firm, then combine with the other ingredients.

6. Carefully pour in the chicken broth and, without breaking up the tofu, deglaze the cooking pot, scraping up any browned bits from the bottom of the pot.

7. Stir in the pad Thai sauce. Add the noodles and submerge them into the liquid.

8. Lock the lid and close the pressure valve. Cook for 1 minute on High Pressure. When the beep sounds, wait 5 minutes, then release the remaining pressure. Do not turn off the pot.

9. Remove the lid and stir in the shrimp. Replace the lid on the cooker, but do not lock it in place. When the Keep Warm time on the pot reaches 10 minutes, remove the lid and stir.

10. Serve the pad Thai topped with the garnishes.

Vietnamese Pork Thịt Nu'ó'ng Rice Bowl

PREP: 20 MIN.
COOK: 3 MIN.
YIELD: 4 SERVINGS

My favorite Vietnamese restaurant is in Reseda, California, and when I lived nearby, I was a frequent patron. I love their cold noodle salad, and this recipe is inspired by it.

Marinade

3 lemongrass stalks, white parts only, woody, green, grassy blades and loose dry outer layer removed
3 large garlic cloves, peeled
2 shallots
3 tablespoons (45 ml) freshly squeezed lime juice
3 tablespoons (45 ml) extra-virgin olive oil
2 teaspoons packed light brown sugar
2 teaspoons granulated sugar
2 teaspoons fish sauce
¼ teaspoon freshly ground black pepper

Pork

1 pound (454 g) boneless pork shoulder, trimmed and cut into 3 x ½-inch (7.5 x 1 cm) slices
12 ounces (340 g) jasmine rice
1¼ cups (300 ml) water

Nuoc Cham (Dipping Sauce)

⅔ cup (160 ml) hot water
¼ cup (60 ml) fish sauce
¼ cup (50 g) sugar
2½ tablespoons (38 ml) freshly squeezed lime juice
2 Thai bird's eye chiles, stemmed and seeded
1 garlic clove, peeled
½ teaspoon Sambal Oelek Ground Fresh Chili Paste
2 tablespoons (14 g) shredded carrot

Bowls

1 cup (70 g) shredded napa cabbage
1 cup (50 g) bean sprouts
Fresh mint leaves
Fresh Thai basil leaves
1 cucumber, peeled and julienned, for garnishing
¾ cup (87 g) đồ chua (pickled daikon and carrots), julienned, for garnishing
Fresh cilantro leaves, for garnishing
Chopped unsalted roasted peanuts, for garnishing
1 scallion, sliced, for garnishing

1. **To make the marinade:** In a food processor, add all the marinade ingredients and process until blended. Transfer to a large resealable plastic bag or airtight container. Add the pork pieces to the marinade, seal the container, and refrigerate overnight.

2. **To make the nuoc cham:** In a food processor, add the hot water, fish sauce, sugar, lime juice, chiles, garlic, and chili paste. Pulse to combine. Transfer to an airtight container and refrigerate overnight.

3. **To make the pork:** In your pressure cooker cooking pot, combine the pork and marinade, rice, and water.

4. Lock the lid and close the pressure valve. Cook for 3 minutes on High Pressure. When the beep sounds, wait 10 minutes, then release the remaining pressure.

5. **To assemble the bowls:** Divide the cabbage, bean sprouts, mint, and basil among four large salad bowls.

6. Fluff the rice and pork, and divide among the prepared bowls.

7. Garnish each bowl with cucumber, đồ chua, and cilantro, and top with crushed peanuts and scallion.

8. Float the shredded carrot on top of the nuoc cham sauce and generously drizzle it on the bowls.

♥ **TOG TIP!**
Craving a delicious banh mi (Vietnamese sandwich)? Omit the rice and water from the recipe, and instead of a rice bowl, pile the meat and veggies onto a good hoagie bun.

Notes

_____

_____

_____

_____

_____

_____

_____

_____

_____

_____

_____

_____

Egg Roll in a Bowl

This bowl has all the taste of an egg roll without the deep-frying. Serve with brown, white, or fried rice.

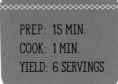

PREP: 15 MIN.
COOK: 1 MIN.
YIELD: 6 SERVINGS

Sauce

7 tablespoons (105 ml) sweet/black soy sauce
5 tablespoons (75 ml) low-sodium soy sauce
½ teaspoon ground white pepper
¼ teaspoon Chinese five-spice powder

Bowls

2 tablespoons (30 ml) extra-virgin olive oil
1 tablespoon (15 ml) pure sesame oil
1 pound (454 g) ground pork, turkey, or chicken
2½ tablespoons (15 g) peeled fresh ginger, minced
2½ tablespoons (25 g) garlic, minced
3 scallions, white parts chopped and green parts sliced, divided
1 celery rib, chopped
1 can (8 ounces, or 227 g) water chestnuts (optional)
3 pounds (1.4 kg) coleslaw mix, divided (see TOG Tip!)
2 pounds (907 g) cleaned raw shrimp, chopped
Cooked rice, for serving
Hoisin sauce, for serving
Sweet and Sour Sauce (page XX)

1. **To make the sauce:** In a small bowl, combine all the sauce ingredients. Set aside.

2. **To make the bowls:** On your pressure cooker, select Sauté or Browning and fully heat the cooking pot.

3. Add the olive and sesame oils to the cooking pot. When they start to sizzle, add the meat. Brown for 2 minutes.

4. Add the ginger and garlic. Sauté until browned. Add the chopped white scallions and celery. Sauté for 1 minute. Turn off the pressure cooker.

5. Add the water chestnuts (if using), half of the coleslaw mix, and half the sauce. Stir to combine.

6. Lock the lid and close the pressure valve. Cook for 1 minute on High Pressure. When the beep sounds, release all the pressure.

7. Select Sauté or Browning, remove the lid, and add the remaining half of the sauce, the shrimp, and the remaining half of the coleslaw mix. Stir for about 1 minute, or until the shrimp are no longer translucent. Stir in the sliced green scallions.

8. Serve over rice and with the hoisin and sweet and sour sauces.

♥ TOG TIP!
To save money, shred the green cabbage yourself, along with 1 carrot.

Chicken Taco Bowls

This one-pot meal with Mexican flair is loved by kids and adults alike.

PREP: 20 MIN.
COOK: 2 MIN.
YIELD: 6 SERVINGS

1 tablespoon (15 ml) extra-virgin olive oil
¾ cup (120 g) onion, chopped
1 large red bell pepper, chopped
3 garlic cloves, minced
2½ cups (600 ml) chicken stock or broth
2½ pounds (1.1 kg) boneless, skinless
   chicken breasts, cut into 2-inch
   (5 cm) chunks
16 ounces (454 g) frozen corn kernels
1 can (15 ounces, or 425 g) black beans,
   drained and rinsed
12 ounces (340 g) jasmine or Calrose
   rice, rinsed
1 packet (1 ounce, or 28 g) taco
   seasoning mix, mild or spicy
   (see TOG Tip!)
2 limes, divided
1 tablespoon (15 ml) sea salt
¼ cup (15 g) fresh cilantro leaves,
   chopped, plus more for garnishing
2 cans (14.5 ounces, or 410 g, each) diced
   tomatoes
Tortilla chips, for serving
Grated Cheddar cheese, for garnishing
Sour cream, for garnishing

1. On your pressure cooker, select Sauté or Browning and fully heat the cooking pot.

2. Add the olive oil and onion to the cooking pot. Sauté for 3 minutes.

3. Add the red bell pepper and sauté for 1 minute.

4. Add the garlic and sauté for 30 seconds.

5. Pour in the chicken broth and deglaze the cooking pot, scraping up any browned bits from the bottom of the pot. Turn off the pressure cooker.

6. Add the chicken, corn, black beans, rice, taco seasoning, the juice of 1 lime, sea salt, and cilantro. Cover everything with the diced tomatoes.

7. Lock the lid and close the pressure valve. Cook for 2 minutes on High Pressure. When the beep sounds, wait 5 minutes, then release the remaining pressure.

8. Remove the lid and stir to combine. Serve with tortilla chips and garnished with cheese, sour cream, cilantro, and lime wedges from the remaining lime.

💜 **TOG TIP!**
Try my Taco Seasoning (page 10), instead of store-bought.

Cuban Black Bean Quinoa Bowls

PREP: 15 MIN.
COOK: 1 MIN.
YIELD: 4 SERVINGS

Homemade Cuban-style black beans (*frijoles negros*) with fresh vegetables and quinoa cooked together in one pot make a delicious and healthy meal.

2 teaspoons extra-virgin olive oil
1 large onion, diced
1 large green bell pepper, diced
1 jalapeño pepper, seeded and diced
1 pound (454 g) fresh Roma tomatoes, diced
2 garlic cloves, minced
2 teaspoons salt
1 teaspoon ground cumin
½ teaspoon freshly ground black pepper
2 limes, divided
1 bay leaf
1 pound (454 g) prepared Frijoles Negros (page 157)
8 ounces (225 g) quinoa, washed (see TOG Tips!)
Handful fresh cilantro leaves, chopped
2 avocados, sliced, for serving

1. On your pressure cooker, select Sauté or Browning and fully heat the cooking pot.

2. Add the olive oil to the cooking pot and swirl to coat the bottom of the pot.

3. Add the onion, green bell pepper, and jalapeño. Sauté for 2 minutes.

4. Add the tomatoes and garlic, and sauté for 30 seconds.

5. Stir in the salt, cumin, black pepper, the juice of 1 lime, and bay leaf. Place the black beans and quinoa on top. Do not stir.

6. Lock the lid and close the pressure valve. Cook for 1 minute on High Pressure. When the beep sounds, wait 10 minutes, then release the remaining pressure.

7. Remove the lid, discard the bay leaf, and stir in the cilantro. Serve with lime wedges from the remaining lime and avocado slices.

♥ TOG TIPS!

To prep the quinoa, place it in a bowl of cold water and wash the seeds with your fingers. Pour the quinoa through a strainer to drain the water.

For a vegan version, prepare the black beans without the ham hock.

Pad See Ew Bowl

PREP: 15 MIN.
COOK: 1 MIN.
YIELD: 4 SERVINGS

Years ago, when I worked in law, my colleagues and I used to order the Thai dish *pad see ew* at least once a week for lunch. I had created my own recipe for the wok or cast-iron pan and now have converted it for the pressure cooker. This recipe moves fast, so make sure to do all the prep work first and set the ingredients next to the pressure cooker.

3 garlic cloves, minced

4½ tablespoons (68 ml) oyster sauce

4½ tablespoons (68 ml) sweet/black soy sauce

2½ tablespoons (38 ml) low-sodium soy sauce

2 tablespoons (30 ml) vegetable oil, divided

1 tablespoon (15 ml) distilled white vinegar

1 tablespoon (15 ml) sugar

1 tablespoon (15 ml) fish sauce

8 ounces (225 g) sirloin or flank steak, thinly sliced against the grain

6 ounces (175 g) rice flake noodles (square), dried

2 large eggs, beaten

1²/₃ cups (400 ml) water

3 stalks gai lan (Chinese broccoli), stems separated from the leaves and stems sliced on the diagonal, divided (see TOG Tip!)

♥ **TOG TIP!**

Gai lan *is on the bitter side, similar in taste to broccoli rabe. If you want to use broccoli rabe instead, add it after the pressure is released.*

1. In a large bowl, whisk together the garlic, oyster sauce, sweet/black soy sauce, low-sodium soy sauce, 1 tablespoon (15 ml) of the vegetable oil, the vinegar, sugar, and fish sauce. Mix in the beef to marinate and set aside.

2. On your pressure cooker, select Sauté or Browning and fully heat the cooking pot.

3. Add the remaining 1 tablespoon (15 ml) vegetable oil and the rice noodles to the cooking pot. Sauté for 1 minute, just to coat the noodles.

4. Push the noodles aside, add the eggs, and scramble until slightly firm. Mix the scrambled eggs into the noodles.

5. Add the beef and marinade to the cooking pot, and stir to combine witht the eggs and noodles.

6. Add the water and deglaze the cooking pot, scraping up any browned bits from the bottom of the pot. Turn off the pressure cooker.

7. Place the gai lan stems on top.

8. Lock the lid and close the pressure valve. Cook for 1 minute on High Pressure. When the beep sounds, wait 5 minutes, then release the remaining pressure.

9. Remove the lid and add the gai lan leaves, stirring until wilted.

INDIAN MEALS

CHICKEN TIKKA MASALA

GHEE *Matar Paneer*

PANEER **AND** MURGH MAKHANI

Chicken Tikka Masala with Butter Rice and Peas

PREP: 35 MIN.
COOK: 4 MIN.
YIELD: 4 SERVINGS

Chicken *tikka masala* is a favorite Indian-restaurant dish that happens to be more British than Indian.

Marinade
¼ cup (60 g) thick Greek Yogurt (page 24)
1 tablespoon (15 ml) kosher salt
1 tablespoon (15 ml) ground coriander
1 tablespoon (15 ml) ground cumin

Tikka Masala
2½ pounds (1.3 kg) boneless, skinless chicken thighs (see TOG Tip!), cut in half
¼ cup (55 g) Simple Ghee (page 93)
1 tablespoon (15 ml) extra-virgin olive oil
1 large onion, diced
2 tablespoons (40 g) Garlic-Ginger Paste (page 10)
¾ cup (180 ml) water or chicken broth, divided
3 tablespoons (18 g) garam masala, divided
1 can (28 ounces, or 794 g) crushed tomatoes
1 tablespoon (15 ml) raw sugar
1 or 2 cinnamon sticks
1 or 2 jalapeño peppers, stemmed and pierced with a sharp knife
¾ to 1 cup (180 to 240 ml) heavy cream, plus more as needed

Butter Rice and Peas
16 ounces (454 g) basmati or jasmine rice, rinsed until the water runs clear
1 teaspoon sea salt
¼ cup (55 g) salted butter
2 cups (475 ml) water
1 cup (130 g) frozen sweet peas, thawed

1. **To make the marinade:** In a large bowl, combine all the marinade ingredients.

2. **To make the tikka masala:** Add the chicken to the marinade and stir to coat. Let marinate for 20 to 30 minutes.

3. On your pressure cooker, select Sauté or Browning and fully heat the cooking pot.

4. Add the ghee and olive oil to the cooking pot.

5. Add the chicken and lightly brown on all sides, about 1 minute total. Add the onion and garlic-ginger paste, and sauté for 30 seconds more.

6. Pour in the water and deglaze the cooking pot, scraping up any browned bits from the bottom of the pot.

7. Stir in 1½ tablespoons (9 g) of the garam masala and the sugar. Pour in the tomatoes and combine thoroughly. Turn off the pressure cooker.

8. Add the cinnamon stick(s) and jalapeño(s), pushing them into the sauce.

9. **To make the butter rice and peas:** In a flat-bottomed, stainless steel pan, combine the rice, sea salt, and butter. Place a long-legged stainless steel trivet into the cooking pot and place the pan with the rice on top. Pour the water into the pan. (It is easier to do after the pan is sitting on the trivet.)

10. Lock the lid and close the pressure valve. Cook for 4 minutes on High Pressure. When the beep sounds, wait 10 minutes, then release remaining pressure.

(continued on next page)

11. Remove the lid, pan, and trivet. Add the peas to the rice and fluff with a fork to combine. Cover the rice to keep it warm.

12. On your pressure cooker, select Sauté or Browning. Stir in the remaining 1½ tablespoons (9 g) garam masala.

13. Simmer for about 5 minutes to thicken the sauce. Stir in the heavy cream and serve with the rice.

🩶 **TOG TIP!**
If using white meat chicken, reduce the cooking time to 2 minutes.

Notes

Simple Ghee

No need to stand at the stove and stir. Use the slow-cooker option on your multi-cooker for the bulk of the time, walk away, and enjoy quality time with your family.

PREP: 1 MIN.
COOK: 2 H. 20 MIN.
YIELD: 1¾ CUPS (392 G)

32 ounces (907 g) unsalted Kerrygold butter

1. Place the butter in the cooking pot.

2. Lock the lid and vent the pressure valve (keep it open). Select Slow Cooker and adjust the temperature to Medium. Set the timer for 2 hours.

3. When the beep sounds, turn off the slow-cook function, remove the lid, and select Sauté or Browning and adjust to the Low setting. Stir the ghee for 15 to 20 minutes, until the solids solidify and fall to the bottom. The solids will begin to caramelize, which is what you want to happen. This is when the clarified butter turns to ghee.

4. Line a strainer with cheesecloth and set aside.

5. When the beep sounds, let the ghee cool almost to room temperature. Place the lined strainer over a glass jar and pour the ghee through the strainer.

6. Cover and store the ghee on the counter or in the refrigerator.

Matar Paneer
(Indian Peas and Cheese in Gravy)

PREP: 20 MIN.
COOK: 5 MIN.
YIELD: 4 SERVINGS

Vegetarian Indian food is in my top three favorite cuisines. The rich sauce and fragrant spices, along with the homemade Paneer (page 96), make for a very comforting and warming meal.

Gravy—Part 1

1½ pounds (24 ounces, or 680 g) diced tomatoes, canned or fresh
⅓ cup (47 g) raw cashews
¼ cup (60 ml) water
6 green cardamom pods, seeds removed and crushed, or ⅓ teaspoon ground cardamom
2 green chiles, chopped
1 medium carrot, chopped
1½ tablespoons (30 g) Garlic-Ginger Paste (page 10)
1½ tablespoons (23 ml) kosher salt
2 teaspoons garam masala, divided
1 cinnamon stick
½ teaspoon Kashmiri chile powder (for color; see TOG Tips!)
½ teaspoon Sambal Oelek Ground Fresh Chili Paste
Perfectly Cooked Pot-in-Pot Rice (page 153; optional)

Gravy—Part 2

8 ounces (225 g) peas, fresh or frozen
¼ cup (55 g) salted butter
¼ to ½ cup (60 to 120 ml) heavy cream
8 ounces (225 g) Paneer cubes (page 96)
1 tablespoon (4 g) fresh cilantro leaves, chopped
1½ teaspoons crushed kasoori methi (dried fenugreek leaves; see TOG Tips!)

1. **To make the gravy—part 1:** In your pressure cooker cooking pot, combine all the gravy part 1 ingredients.

2. If making the rice, place a tall-legged stainless-steel trivet into the pressure cooker cooking pot and place the pan of rice and broth (as instructed in the recipe on page 153) on it.

3. Lock the lid and close the pressure valve. Cook for 5 minutes on High Pressure. When the beep sounds, wait 10 minutes, then release the remaining pressure.

4. Remove the lid and rice, and discard the cinnamon stick. With an immersion blender, blend the gravy until smooth.

5. **To make the gravy—part 2:** On your pressure cooker, select Sauté or Browning. Add the peas and simmer until the gravy begins to thicken. Stir in the butter, heavy cream, and paneer cubes. Stir in the cilantro and kasoori methi.

6. Serve with the rice (if using).

♥ TOG TIPS!

Kashmiri chile powder is mild with a bright red color. It is used in Indian cooking for color, more so than heat.

Kasoori methi adds a subtle flavor. If you cannot find it, add a bit of parsley instead. But I do suggest buying it— an ounce (28 g) will last a long time.

Paneer
(Indian Cottage Cheese)

PREP: 20 MIN.
COOK: 1 MIN.
YIELD: 1 POUND (454 G)

Used in so many Indian recipes, paneer is just fresh curdled cheese, which has had the liquid pressed out of it with a vice or pressing it with a weight. Similar to farmer cheese, paneer does not melt and is firm. It is also delicious pan-fried and enjoyed as a snack.

1½ quarts (1.4 L) whole milk
¼ cup (60 ml) distilled white vinegar
¼ cup (60 ml) water

💙 **TOG TIP!**
If using the paneer in savory dishes, add 1 teaspoon salt during crumbling, if desired.

1. Line a colander with butter muslin or cheesecloth and set aside.

2. In your pressure cooker cooking pot, combine the milk, white vinegar, and water.

3. Lock the lid and close the pressure valve. Cook for 1 minute on High Pressure. When the beep sounds, wait 10 minutes, then release any remaining pressure.

4. Strain the paneer in the lined colander to separate the milk solids from the whey. Grab the ends of the cloth and rinse the cheese under cool water to remove the vinegar taste. Squeeze out all the water from the paneer.

5. Place the wrapped cheese on a plate and firmly press out any remaining water, using a heavy weight or a tofu press.

6. Remove the paneer from the cloth and crumble it. Knead until it forms a moldable "dough," which will give you a softer, smoother texture.

7. Shape the paneer into a square or rectangle, ½ or ¾ inch (1 to 2 cm) thick, and wrap tightly in fresh butter muslin or cheesecloth. Press the paneer again, to remove any excess water. Refrigerate the wrapped paneer for at least 4 hours.

8. Remove the paneer from the cloth and cut into cubes or strips. Use immediately or keep refrigerated in an airtight container for up to 1 week.

Murgh Makhani
(Indian Butter Chicken)

PREP: 1 H. 20 MIN.
COOK: 3 MIN.
YIELD: 4 SERVINGS

This tender chicken in a rich tomato sauce gets its buttery flavor from the cashew paste, and the chicken "cuts like butter."

Marinade

¾ cup (175 g) full-fat Greek Yogurt (page 24)

1½ tablespoons (30 g) Garlic-Ginger Paste (page 10)

1 tablespoon (15 ml) freshly squeezed lime juice

2 teaspoons garam masala

Creamy Tomato Sauce

2 teaspoons garam masala, divided

1 can (28 ounces, or 794 g) whole tomatoes

¼ cup (35 g) raw cashews

2 tablespoons (28 g) salted butter

1 tablespoon (20 g) Garlic-Ginger Paste (page XX)

2 teaspoons sea salt

1 teaspoon ground cumin

½ teaspoon ground coriander

¼ teaspoon dried fenugreek

¼ teaspoon ground turmeric

¼ teaspoon cayenne pepper

¼ teaspoon chili powder

Chicken

2 pounds (907 g) boneless, skinless chicken thighs, halved

3 tablespoons (42 g) Simple Ghee (page 93)

½ cup (120 ml) chicken broth

1. **To make the marinade:** In a large resealable plastic bag or large bowl, combine all the marinade ingredients. Add the chicken to the marinade, seal the bag or cover the bowl with plastic wrap, and refrigerate for 1 hour.

2. **To make the creamy tomato sauce:** In a blender, add 1 teaspoon of the garam masala and the rest of the creamy tomato sauce ingredients. Process until smooth. Set aside.

3. **To make the chicken:** On your pressure cooker, select Sauté or Browning and fully heat the cooking pot .

4. Add the ghee to the cooking pot.

5. Working in batches, brown the chicken on all sides, about 5 seconds per side, and transfer to a plate.

6. Pour in the chicken broth and deglaze the cooking pot, scraping up any browned bits from the bottom of the pot. Turn off the pressure cooker.

7. Pour the creamy tomato sauce into the cooking pot and carefully add the chicken to the sauce.

8. Lock the lid and close the pressure valve. Cook for 3 minutes on High Pressure. When the beep sounds, wait 10 minutes, then release the remaining pressure.

(continued on next page)

9. Remove the lid and stir in the remaining 1 teaspoon garam masala.

10. For a thicker sauce, on your pressure cooker, select Sauté or Browning and adjust to Low. Simmer until the sauce reaches desired consistency (see TOG Tip!).

💙 **TOG TIP!**
For a richer sauce, add 2 tablespoons (28 g) of butter after the pressure is released in step 8.

Notes

_____

_____

_____

_____

_____

_____

_____

_____

_____

_____

_____

_____

SOUPS AND STEWS

CREAMY CARROT-GINGER SOUP

CHICKEN MARSALA MUSHROOM SOUP

ZUPPA • *Ratatouille*

TOSCANA GALBITANG

AMERICANA WEDDING

CHILI CON CARNE

SEAFOOD CORN CHOWDER

Creamy Carrot-Ginger Soup

Warm up with a fragrant bowl of this zingy soup on a chilly day.

PREP: 20 MIN.
COOK: 6 MIN.
YIELD: 6 SERVINGS

1 tablespoon (15 ml) coconut oil
2 pounds (907 g) carrots, roughly
    chopped
1 large sweet onion, roughly chopped
4 garlic cloves, minced
3-inch (7.5 cm) piece fresh ginger,
    peeled and minced
1½ quarts (1.4 L) vegetable or chicken
    broth
2 tablespoons (40 g) honey
1 tablespoon (15 ml) kosher salt
1 teaspoon Sambal Oelek Ground
    Fresh Chili Paste
½ teaspoon ground turmeric
½ teaspoon ground cumin
½ teaspoon ground cinnamon
½ teaspoon freshly ground black pepper
½ cup (120 ml) coconut cream

1. On your pressure cooker, select Sauté or Browning and fully heat the cooking pot.

2. Add the coconut oil, carrots, and onion to the cooking pot. Sauté for about 3 minutes, until the onion begins to brown.

3. Add the garlic and ginger, and sauté for 1 minute more.

4. Pour in the vegetable broth and deglaze the cooking pot, scraping up any browned bits from the bottom of the pot.

5. Add the honey, kosher salt, chili paste, turmeric, cumin, cinnamon, and black pepper.

6. Lock the lid and close the pressure valve. Cook for 6 minutes on High Pressure. When the beep sounds, wait 10 minutes, then release the remaining pressure.

7. Using an immersion blender, process the soup until very smooth. Taste and adjust the salt, pepper, and chili paste as needed.

8. Ladle into bowls and swirl each serving with a drizzle of the coconut cream (see TOG Tip!).

💜 **TOG TIP!**

For a richer soup, add a dollop of Greek Yogurt (page 24) or sour cream to each bowl.

Chicken Marsala Mushroom Soup

PREP: 25 MIN.
COOK: 3 MIN.
YIELD: 8 SERVINGS

This yummy combination of chicken Marsala and mushroom soup makes for a hearty meal. Serve it with a loaf of sourdough bread.

4 cups (960 ml) plus 5 tablespoons (75 ml) water, divided

5 heaping teaspoons chicken base

3 ounces (85 g) prosciutto

2 teaspoons extra-virgin olive oil

¼ cup (55 g) salted butter

3 large shallots, chopped

1¼ pounds (567 g) cremini mushrooms

4 ounces (115 g) fancy mushrooms (such as king trumpet, enoki, morels, porcini, chanterelle)

¾ cup (180 ml) dry Marsala wine (not cooking wine), divided

2 garlic cloves, sliced

2 teaspoons kosher salt

¼ teaspoon freshly ground black pepper

⅛ teaspoon ground marjoram

1½ pounds (680 g) boneless, skinless chicken breasts

2 sprigs fresh thyme

1 tablespoon (15 ml) potato starch

Freshly shaved Asiago or Parmesan cheese, for garnishing

Fresh parsley leaves, for garnishing (optional)

1. Line a plate with paper towels and set aside.

2. In a medium bowl, stir together 4 cups (960 ml) of the water and the chicken base. Set aside.

3. In the pressure cooker cooking pot, combine the prosciutto and the remaining 5 tablespoons (75 ml) water. Select Sauté or Browning and cook for about 3 minutes, until the water almost evaporates.

4. Add the olive oil to the cooking pot. Use a spatula to break up the prosciutto, cooking until crisp, about 6 minutes. Be careful not to let the prosciutto burn.

5. Transfer the prosciutto to the paper towel–lined plate to cool. Chop into pieces with a sharp knife and set aside.

6. Add the butter to the cooking pot and swirl it to melt.

7. Add the shallots and mushrooms. Cook until the shallots are soft and the liquid evaporates, about 3 minutes.

8. Add ½ cup (120 ml) of the Marsala and the garlic. Sauté for 5 minutes.

9. Stir in the remaining ¼ cup (60 ml) Marsala, the salt, black pepper, and marjoram. Bring to a simmer.

10. Stir in the chicken broth and add the chicken and thyme to the cooking pot.

11. Lock the lid and close the pressure valve. Cook for 3 minutes on High Pressure. When the beep sounds, wait 10 minutes, then release the remaining pressure.

12. Remove the lid and discard the thyme. Transfer the chicken to a cutting board.

13. Using a heat-resistant cup, transfer ½ cup (120 ml) cooking liquid to a small bowl and whisk in the potato starch. Pour this slurry back into the soup and stir to combine.

14. Use an immersion blender to blend the soup until smooth.

15. Cut the chicken into bite-size pieces and return it to the soup.

16. Ladle the soup into bowls and top with the shaved cheese and crispy prosciutto. Garnish with parsley (if using).

Notes

Ratatouille

Ratatouille brings back memories of my time rehearsing for *Sweatin' to the Oldies 3* with Richard Simmons. After rehearsal, castmates frequently gathered for dinner at a cute little 1950s diner in Beverly Hills, and their ratatouille was my favorite.

PREP: 30 MIN.
COOK: 3 MIN.
YIELD: 6 SERVINGS

¼ cup (60 ml) extra-virgin olive oil, divided
1 pound (454 g) onions, roughly chopped
1 garlic head, peeled and minced
⅛ teaspoon fennel seeds, crushed
¼ cup (60 ml) red wine vinegar
2 pounds (32 ounces, or 907 g) Roma tomatoes (fresh or canned), quartered
1 large red bell pepper, roughly chopped
1 large green bell pepper, roughly chopped
1 pound (454 g) zucchini, cut into 1-inch (2.5 cm) chunks
1 pound (454 g) eggplant, cut into 1-inch (2.5 cm) chunks
2 to 3 teaspoons kosher salt
½ teaspoon Sambal Oelek Ground Fresh Chili Paste or pinch red pepper flakes
1 teaspoon dried oregano, crumbled
½ teaspoon dried thyme, crumbled
¼ teaspoon ground coriander
¼ cup (10 g) fresh basil leaves, chopped

1. On your pressure cooker, select Sauté or Browning and fully heat the cooking pot.

2. Add 3 tablespoons (45 ml) of the olive oil and the onions to the cooking pot. Sauté for 3 minutes.

3. Add the garlic and fennel seeds. Sauté for 30 seconds more.

4. Pour in the red wine vinegar and deglaze the cooking pot, scraping up any browned bits from the bottom of the pot.

5. Add the tomatoes, red and green bell peppers, zucchini, eggplant, kosher salt, chili paste, oregano, thyme, and coriander.

6. Lock the lid and close the pressure valve. Cook for 3 minutes on High Pressure. When the beep sounds, wait 10 minutes, then release the remaining pressure.

7. Remove the lid and stir in the remaining 1 tablespoon (15 ml) olive oil and the basil (See TOG Tips!).

💜 **TOG TIPS!**

Serve with shaved Parmesan cheese or crumbled feta cheese on top, if desired.

This dish is great served cold or warm, over rice, barley, or quinoa.

Americana Wedding Soup

Chewy meatballs and dainty pink radishes with their bright green tops make for a fun and interesting meal for kids and adults alike.

PREP: 25 MIN.
COOK: 5 MIN.
YIELD: 6 SERVINGS

Meatballs

½ cup (45 g) grated Asiago cheese
½ cup (100 g) pearl barley or farro (not instant)
¼ cup (40 g) onion
¼ cup (15 g) fresh parsley leaves
1 large egg
1 garlic clove, minced
1 teaspoon kosher salt
½ teaspoon dried basil
½ teaspoon freshly ground black pepper
⅛ teaspoon fennel seeds, finely crushed
1 pound (454 g) ground beef and/or pork

Soup

1 tablespoon (15 ml) extra-virgin olive oil
1 celery rib, finely diced
1 medium onion, finely diced
2 garlic cloves, minced
¼ cup (60 ml) dry white wine
10 cups (2.4 L) low-sodium chicken broth
8 ounces (225 g) carrots, peeled and sliced ½ inch (13 mm) thick
1 pound (454 g) small red radishes, trimmed, leaving ¼ inch (6 mm) of green stem, and halved lengthwise from stem to end
2 teaspoons kosher salt, plus more as needed
1 cup escarole (36 g), Swiss chard (36 g), or arugula (20 g), roughly chopped
1 large egg, well beaten

1. **To make the meatballs:** In a food processor, combine the cheese, barley, onion, parsley, egg, garlic, kosher salt, basil, black pepper, and fennel seeds. Process until well combined. Add the beef and pulse a couple of times to combine. Form the mixture into 38 meatballs. Set aside.

2. **To make the soup:** On your pressure cooker, select Sauté or Browning and fully heat the cooking pot.

3. Add the olive oil and celery to the cooking pot. Sauté for 3 minutes.

4. Add the onion and garlic, and sauté for 30 seconds more.

5. Pour in the white wine and deglaze the cooking pot, scraping up any browned bits on the bottom of the pot. Simmer for 2 minutes. Stir in the chicken broth. Carefully add the meatballs, carrots, radishes, and kosher salt.

6. Lock the lid and close the pressure valve. Cook for 5 minutes on High Pressure. When the beep sounds, wait 15 minutes, then release the remaining pressure.

7. Remove the lid and stir in the greens.

8. With a fork, stir the soup in a circular motion. Slowly drizzle the beaten egg into the middle of the pot while slowly stirring to form thin strands of egg. Taste the broth and adjust the salt and pepper, if needed.

Galbitang *(Korean Kalbi Soup)*

PREP: 20 MIN.
COOK: 35 MIN.
YIELD: 4 SERVINGS

The soup that is a meal! *Galbitang*, with its melt-in-your-mouth beef short ribs in a rich, beefy broth and glass noodles, is a very popular soup in Korean households. Enjoy with a halved Hard-Boiled Egg (page 21) in each bowl.

4 pounds (1.8 kg) beef bone-in short ribs
3 quarts (2.8 L) water
1 tablespoon (17 g) beef base
1 large onion, unpeeled and halved
½ large Korean radish, halved
1 garlic head, peeled
   and halved (10 to 12 cloves)
4-inch (10 cm) piece fresh ginger,
   peeled and minced
2 tablespoons (30 ml) fish sauce
1 tablespoon (15 ml) soy sauce
1 tablespoon (15 g) packed light brown
   sugar (see TOG Tips!)
2 teaspoons kosher salt
1 teaspoon sesame oil
1 teaspoon Sambal Oelek Ground Fresh
   Chili Paste
1 teaspoon freshly ground black pepper
6 scallions, chopped
8 ounces (225 g) glass noodles
1 large carrot, julienned

1. Rinse the ribs under cold water to remove any bone shards (see TOG Tips!).

2. Add the ribs, water, beef base, onion, radish, garlic, ginger, fish sauce, soy sauce, brown sugar, salt, sesame oil, chili paste, and black pepper to the cooking pot.

3. Lock the lid and close the pressure valve. Cook for 35 minutes on High Pressure. When the beep sounds, wait 15 minutes, then release the remaining pressure.

4. Remove the lid and transfer the ribs and radish from the cooking liquid to a cutting board. Skim off excess fat from the liquid and strain the broth through a fine-mesh strainer.

5. Pour the strained broth back into the cooking pot and select Sauté or Browning. Add the glass noodles and simmer for 2 minutes, or until soft. Stir in the scallions.

6. Divide the ribs, noodles, and scallions among 4 large soup bowls and ladle the broth over them. Slice the radish into thin strips and divide among the bowls. Top each with some carrot.

♥ TOG TIPS!

The brown sugar adds a touch of sweetness to the soup.

Don't skip step 1, as you want to make sure to rinse away any bone shards.

Chili con Carne

This is a classic, flavorful chili made with beans and a touch of heat.

PREP: 15 MIN.
COOK: 10 MIN.
YIELD: 6 SERVINGS

3 tablespoons (45 ml) extra-virgin olive oil
1½ pounds (680 g) ground beef
1 large onion, diced
1 large red bell pepper, diced
1 large jalapeño pepper, stemmed, seeded, and finely diced
2 tablespoons (20 g) garlic, minced
1 tablespoon (15 ml) chili powder
1½ teaspoons ground cumin
1½ teaspoons sea salt
1 teaspoon dried oregano
½ teaspoon freshly ground black pepper
1 tablespoon (15 ml) fish sauce (see TOG Tip!)
2 teaspoons cocoa powder (see TOG Tip!)
1 can (28 ounces, or 794 g) whole peeled tomatoes
1¾ cups (425 ml) water
1 can (14 ounces, or 395 g) black beans, rinsed and drained
1 can (14 ounces, or 395 g) kidney beans, rinsed and drained
1 tablespoon (15 ml) Worcestershire sauce

1. On your pressure cooker, select Sauté or Browning and fully heat the cooking pot.

2. Add the olive oil, followed by the ground beef, to the cooking pot. Cook for 3 to 4 minutes, until the beef is slightly browned, breaking it up well with a wooden spoon. Drain off the fat.

3. Add the onion, red bell pepper, and jalapeño. Sauté for 3 minutes.

4. Add the garlic, chili powder, cumin, kosher salt, oregano, black pepper, fish sauce, cocoa powder, tomatoes, water, black beans, kidney beans, and Worcestershire sauce. Combine.

5. Lock the lid and close the pressure value. Cook for 10 minutes on High Pressure. When the beep sounds, wait 10 minutes, then release the remaining pressure.

6. Serve as is or select Sauté or Browning and simmer for a thicker chili.

♥ **TOG TIP!**
The fish sauce and cocoa powder are flavor boosters.

Zuppa Toscana
(Sausage and Kale Soup)

PREP: 20 MIN.
COOK: 5 MIN.
YIELD: 4 SERVINGS

For a low-carb option, replace the potato with radishes, which lose their bitter taste when cooked and make a great, healthy alternative.

4 bacon slices, roughly chopped

1 medium onion, roughly chopped

1 pound (454 g) hot Italian sausage, casings removed

4 garlic cloves, minced

3 large potatoes, unpeeled and sliced ¼ inch (6 mm) thick

1½ quarts (1.4 L) chicken stock or broth

¼ cup (60 ml) water

2 cups (134 g) fresh kale chiffonade (ribbons)

1 cup (240 ml) heavy cream

1. On your pressure cooker, select Sauté or Browning and fully heat the cooking pot.

2. Add the bacon to the cooking pot and cook for about 5 minutes, until crisp. Transfer the bacon to a paper towel–lined plate and drain all but 2 teaspoons of the grease from the pot.

3. Add the onion to the bacon grease in the cooking pot. Sauté for 3 minutes.

4. Add the sausage and cook for about 5 minutes, breaking it up with the back of a spoon, until browned.

5. Add the garlic and sauté for 1 minute more.

6. Turn off the pressure cooker and drain out any excess grease, if necessary.

7. Add the potatoes, chicken broth, and water.

8. Lock the lid and close the pressure valve. Cook for 5 minutes on High Pressure. When the beep sounds, wait 10 minutes, then release the remaining pressure.

9. Remove the lid and stir in the kale, stirring until wilted.

10. Stir in the heavy cream. Serve topped with the bacon.

Seafood Corn Chowder

PREP: 15 MIN.
COOK: 7 MIN.
YIELD: 4 SERVINGS

Make sure to have plenty of bread on hand with this chowder, as you are going to want to sop up the delicious broth.

¼ cup (55 g) salted butter
1 cup (160 g) onion, chopped
3 garlic cloves, minced
¼ cup (60 ml) dry sherry
4 cups (32 ounces, or 946 ml) chicken broth
2 cups (280 g) corn kernels
3 large carrots, chopped into 1½-inch (3.5 cm) chunks
8 ounces (225 g) cremini mushrooms, halved
2 cups (200 g) string beans, halved
1 pound (454 g) potatoes, peeled and cubed
2 bay leaves
2½ teaspoons ground celery seed
2½ teaspoons dry mustard
2 teaspoons dried parsley flakes
1½ teaspoons sea salt
¾ teaspoon paprika
³/₈ teaspoon ground ginger
¼ teaspoon freshly ground black pepper
¼ teaspoon plus ⅛ teaspoon ground allspice
⅛ teaspoon plus pinch ground cardamom
⅛ teaspoon plus pinch ground cinnamon
⅛ teaspoon white pepper
⅛ teaspoon red pepper flakes
Juice of ½ lemon
1 pound (454 g) mixed seafood (such as shrimp, scallops, fish, crab, oysters, mussels, clams)
½ cup (120 ml) heavy or whipping cream

1. On your pressure cooker, select Sauté or Browning and fully heat the cooking pot.

2. Add the butter, followed by the onion and garlic, to the cooking pot. Sauté for 3 minutes, or until the onion begins to brown slightly. Turn off the pressure cooker.

3. Pour in the sherry and deglaze the cooking pot, scraping up any browned bits from the bottom of the pot.

4. Add the chicken broth, corn, carrots, mushrooms, string beans, and potatoes, along with the bay leaves, celery seed, mustard, parsley, sea salt, paprika, ginger, black pepper, allspice, cardamom, cinnamon, white pepper, and red pepper flakes, and lemon juice.

5. Lock the lid and close the pressure valve. Cook for 7 minutes on High Pressure. When the beep sounds, allow a full natural pressure release (about 15 minutes).

6. Remove the lid, select Sauté or Browning, and add the seafood, stirring until fully cooked.

7. Stir in the cream and heat through before serving.

💙 **TOG TIP!**
The potatoes will break apart and act as a thickening agent.

CHINESE FAVORITES

CHAR SIU   HOT & SOUR SOUP

Orange Pepper Chicken

BEEF AND BROCCOLI
PORK TENDERLOIN

Char Siu (Chinese Barbecue Pork)

There is a hole-in-the-wall Chinese restaurant in Florida that makes the best *char siu*. *Char siu* is a sweet and heavily spiced pork, with cinnamon and honey being the top notes.

PREP: 1 DAY AHEAD
COOK: 4 MIN.
YIELD: 4 SERVINGS

Marinade

1 tablespoon (20 g) honey
1 tablespoon (15 ml) sugar
1 tablespoon (15 ml) oyster sauce
1 cinnamon stick
1½ teaspoons Shaoxing wine
1 teaspoon fish sauce
1 teaspoon soy sauce
½ teaspoon sesame oil
½ teaspoon salt
½ teaspoon ground white pepper

Pork

1 pound (454 g) boneless pork shoulder or pork belly, skin removed, trimmed, and sliced into ½-inch thick (13 mm) strips
12 ounces (340 g) jasmine rice, rinsed until the water runs clear
2 cups (475 ml) water, divided
Sliced scallions, for garnish

Basting Sauce

3 tablespoons (60 g) honey
2 tablespoons (30 ml) soy sauce
1 tablespoon (15 g) packed light brown sugar
Pinch ground cinnamon

1. **To make the marinade:** In a large airtight container or large resealable plastic bag, add all the marinade ingredients and whisk to blend.

2. **To make the pork:** Add the pork slices to the marinade. Seal the container and refrigerate overnight to marinate.

3. In the pressure cooker cooking pot, combine the pork, marinade, and ½ cup (120 ml) of the water. Place a tall-legged stainless-steel trivet over the pork and place a flat-bottom pan on the trivet. Add the rice and remaining 1½ cups (360 ml) of water to the pan.

4. Lock the lid and close the pressure valve. Cook for 4 minutes on High Pressure. When the beep sounds, wait 10 minutes, then release the remaining pressure.

5. Remove the rice, cover to keep warm, and set aside.

6. **To make the basting sauce:** In a small bowl, whisk together all the basting sauce ingredients and char the pork in the oven or an air fryer. In the oven: Remove the pork from the cooking pot and place it on a rimmed baking sheet. Baste the pork with the sauce. Broil until the sauce begins to caramelize. Flip and baste the other side. Cook until slightly charred. In an air fryer: Remove the pork from the cooking pot, coat it with the sauce, and place it in the air fryer at 375°F (190°C). Shake often and cook until slightly charred.

7. Divide the rice among 4 bowls, top with pork, and garnish with sliced scallions.

Hot and Sour Soup

Hot and sour soup is a classic Chinese soup. My vegetarian version is made with wood ear mushrooms, lily flowers, and tofu. It's guaranteed to clear your sinuses!

PREP: 45 MIN.
COOK: 5 MIN.
YIELD: 4 SERVINGS

1 ounce (28 g) dried wood ear mushrooms, rehydrated (see TOG Tips!)

½ ounce (15 g) dried lily flowers, rehydrated (see TOG Tips!)

14 ounces (396 g) firm tofu, cubed

½ cup (75 g) canned bamboo shoots

2½ quarts (2.4 L) vegetable broth

¼ cup (60 ml) dark soy sauce

1 tablespoon (10 g) garlic, grated (about 3 cloves)

2-inch (5 cm) piece fresh ginger, peeled and grated

1 teaspoon Sambal Oelek Ground Fresh Chili Paste

3 large eggs

1 teaspoon pure sesame oil, divided

1¼ cups (60 ml) Chinkiang black vinegar

1 to 1½ teaspoons ground white pepper

6 scallions, thinly sliced

Fresh cilantro leaves, for garnishing (optional)

1. Drain the liquid from the mushrooms. Remove and discard the stems and hard nubs, and thinly slice the mushrooms.

2. Drain the lily flowers, rinse, and halve.

3. In the pressure cooker cooking pot, combine the sliced mushrooms, lily flowers, tofu, bamboo shoots, vegetable broth, soy sauce, garlic, ginger, and chili paste.

4. Lock the lid and close the pressure valve. Cook for 5 minutes on High Pressure. When the beep sounds, wait 10 minutes, then release the remaining pressure.

5. Turn off the pressure cooker and select Sauté or Browning. Crack the eggs into a cup and add a couple drops of sesame oil. Whisk well. When the soup begins to bubble, pour the eggs into the middle of the cooking pot. Wait a few seconds, and in a circular motion, slowly stir the soup—just a couple times.

6. Turn the pressure cooker to Keep Warm and add the remaining sesame oil, the vinegar, and white pepper.

7. Drop in the scallions. Serve with a garnish of fresh cilantro (if using).

♥ **TOG TIPS!**

Cremini mushrooms (8 ounces, or 225 g) may be substituted for the wood ear mushrooms but will not produce the same result.

To rehydrate the mushrooms and lily flowers, place the mushrooms in a medium-size bowl and the lily flowers in a small bowl. Cover each with hot water and let soak for 30 minutes.

Orange Pepper Chicken

This is a moist, juicy, and tender chicken in a lovely, sweet pepper sauce. This recipe was a revolutionary one for me, as it was the first time that I incorporated my proprietary technique using potato starch (page 8), which always renders chicken tender and moist, and not rubbery.

PREP: 20 MIN.
COOK: 5 MIN.
YIELD: 4 SERVINGS

Sauce
1 cup (240 ml) chicken broth
½ cup (142 g) frozen orange juice concentrate
5 garlic cloves, minced
3 tablespoons (45 ml) sweet/black soy sauce
1 tablespoon (15 ml) low-sodium soy sauce
¼ teaspoon Chinese five-spice powder
1 teaspoon Sambal Oelek Ground Fresh Chili Paste (optional)

Chicken
2½ pounds (1.1 kg) boneless, skinless chicken breasts, cut into 2-inch (5 cm) chunks and patted dry
¼ cup (45 g) potato starch
1 teaspoon TOG House Seasoning (page 10)
¼ teaspoon True Orange Ginger (see TOG Tip!)
1 tablespoon (14 g) Simple Ghee (page 93) or other oil (15 ml)
3 large carrots, cut into 1-inch (2.5 cm) chunks
1 large onion, cut into 1-inch (2.5 cm) chunks,
1 medium orange bell pepper, cut into 1-inch (2.5 cm) chunks
1 medium green bell pepper, cut into 1-inch (2.5 cm) chunks

Rice
12 ounces (340 g) jasmine rice or Calrose rice, rinsed until the water runs clear
1½ cups (360 ml) water

Add-ins
¼ cup (71 g) frozen orange juice concentrate
½ cup (85 g) pineapple chunks (optional)
½ bell pepper, diced, for garnishing

1. **To make the sauce:** In a large glass measuring cup or bowl, whisk together the sauce ingredients and chili paste (if using). Set aside.

2. **To make the chicken:** Place the chicken in a large bowl. Sprinkle the potato starch over the chicken and add the house seasoning and True Orange Ginger. Combine well to coat the chicken.

3. On your pressure cooker, select Sauté or Browning and fully heat the cooking pot.

4. Add the ghee to the cooking pot. Shake off any excess potato starch from the chicken and place it in the cooking pot.

5. Sear the chicken for 2 seconds per side to lightly brown on all sides.

6. Add the carrots, onion, and orange and green bell peppers. Stir to combine.

7. Turn off the pressure cooker and pour the sauce into the pot. Gently stir to combine.

8. **To make the rice:** Place a tall-legged stainless steel trivet into the cooking pot and place a round rice pan on top. Add the rinsed rice and water to the pan.

9. Lock the lid and close the pressure valve. Cook for 5 minutes on High Pressure. When the beep sounds, wait 10 minutes, then release the remaining pressure.

10. Remove the lid, rice, and trivet. Fluff the rice with a fork.

11. **To incorporate the add-ins:** On your pressure cooker, select Sauté or Browning. Add in the orange juice concentrate and pineapple chunks (if using). Stir to combine. Cook for 2 minutes. Turn off the pressure cooker.

12. Serve garnished with the diced bell pepper.

♥ **TOG TIP!**
True Orange Ginger is a citrus-based seasoning that adds a huge flavor boost. If you do not have it, substitute 1 teaspoon of grated orange zest and a pinch of ground ginger.

Notes

_____

_____

_____

_____

_____

_____

_____

_____

Beef and Broccoli

Skip the Chinese takeout and make it yourself. In under an hour, you will be enjoying beef and broccoli.

PREP: 15 MIN.
COOK: 4 MIN.
YIELD: 4 SERVINGS

Sauce

½ cup (120 ml) sweet/black soy sauce
¼ cup (60 ml) low-sodium soy sauce
2 tablespoons (30 ml) fish sauce
1 tablespoon (15 ml) pure sesame oil
5 garlic cloves, minced
3 dried red chile peppers (see TOG Tips!)

Beef and Broccoli

2½ pounds (1.1 kg) flank, skirt, or flap steak, thinly sliced against the grain (see TOG Tips!)
½ teaspoon Chinese five-spice powder
2 tablespoons (30 ml) potato starch
1 tablespoon (15 ml) peanut or extra-virgin olive oil
1 medium onion, finely diced
½ cup (120 ml) beef broth
12 ounces (340 g) jasmine rice
1½ cups (350 ml) water
1 pound (454 g) broccoli florets
2 teaspoons toasted sesame oil

♥ TOG TIPS!

For a less spicy version, add the red chile peppers when you add the broccoli in step 8.

When simmering the sauce in step 8, add thinly sliced carrots, mushrooms, and water chestnuts, if you desire.

1. **To make the sauce:** In a large bowl, add all the marinade ingredients and whisk to blend. Set aside.

2. **To make the beef and broccoli:** In a medium bowl, add the sliced beef, Chinese five-spice powder, and potato starch. Mix to coat the beef.

3. On your pressure cooker, select Sauté or Browning and fully heat the cooking pot.

4. Add the peanut oil and beef to the cooking pot and sauté the beef for 10 seconds on each side. Add the, onion, broth, and sauce, and mix through to combine, scraping up any brown bits from the bottom of the pot. Turn off the pressure cooker.

5. Place a tall-legged stainless steel trivet into the pressure cooker cooking pot. In a flat-bottom, stainless steel pan, combine the rice and water. Place the pan on the trivet.

6. Lock the lid and close the pressure valve. Cook for 4 minutes on High Pressure. When the beep sounds, wait 10 minutes, then release the remaining pressure.

7. Remove the lid, rice, and trivet. Quickly cover the rice with aluminum foil to finish steaming.

8. On your pressure cooker, select Sauté or Browning and add the broccoli to the pot. Simmer until the broccoli reaches desired tenderness. Turn off the pressure cooker.

9. Drizzle the sesame oil over the top and serve over the rice.

Sweet and Spicy Pork Tenderloin Medallions

PREP: 35 MINUTES
COOK: 1 MIN.
YIELD: 6 SERVINGS

Spicy and sweet, with a slight kick, this Chinese-style pork tenderloin will melt in your mouth. Serve it over fluffy rice.

2 pork tenderloins, silverskin removed and sliced into 1-inch-thick (2.5 cm) medallions (see TOG Tip!)
¼ cup (60 ml) soy sauce
¼ cup (63 g) hoisin sauce
¼ cup (80 g) honey
¼ cup (60 ml) Shaoxing wine
3 tablespoons (45 g) packed dark brown sugar
2 garlic cloves, minced
1-inch (2.5 cm) piece fresh ginger, peeled and minced
1 tablespoon (15 ml) fish sauce
¾ teaspoon Chinese five-spice powder
½ teaspoon sesame oil
½ teaspoon dry mustard
½ teaspoon Sambal Oelek Ground Fresh Chili Paste
2 scallions, sliced
Cooked rice, for serving (optional)

1. Place the pork in a large resealable plastic bag or airtight container.

2. In a medium bowl, whisk together the soy sauce, hoisin sauce, honey, wine, brown sugar, garlic, ginger, fish sauce, five-spice powder, sesame oil, mustard, and chili paste. Pour over the pork, seal the container, and refrigerate for at least 30 minutes or up to overnight to marinate.

3. Place the pork and marinade into the pressure cooker cooking pot.

4. Lock the lid and close the pressure valve. Cook for 1 minute on High Pressure. When the beep sounds, wait 10 minutes, then release the remaining pressure.

5. Serve over warm rice (if using) and garnish with scallions.

♥ **TOG TIP!**
Pork tenderloin is very lean and a different cut of meat than pork loin. For pork loin, add 1 minute cook time; for pork shoulder, add 4 minutes cook time.

JEWISH FAVORITES

SHABBOS BRUNCH BLINTZ SOUFFLÉ

PASSOVER VEGETABLE MATZO LASAGNA

TZIMMES *Gefilte Fish*

GRANDMA ROSE'S LUCHEN KUGEL

MATZO BALL SOUP

AND *Sweet-and-Sour Stuffed Cabbage*

Shabbos Brunch Blintz Soufflé

PREP: 10 MIN.
COOK: 30 MIN.
YIELD: 6 SERVINGS

This kosher dairy soufflé is usually found at the Shabbos brunch table, along with good friends and good stories.

Blintzes

¼ cup (55 g) salted butter, melted
12 frozen cheese or fruit-flavored blintzes
1½ cups (350 ml) water, for the
  cooking pot

Soufflé

5 large eggs
1½ cups (345 g) sour cream
¼ cup (50 g) sugar
2 tablespoons (30 ml) freshly squeezed
  orange juice
2 teaspoons vanilla extract

Topping

1 recipe Berry Compote (page 13)

1. **To make the blintzes:** Place the melted butter in a 1½-quart (1.4 L) casserole dish and tilt the dish so the butter covers the bottom. Roll the blintzes in the butter and arrange them to fit in the dish (see TOG Tip!).

2. **To make the soufflé:** In a food processor or heavy-duty blender, combine all the soufflé ingredients and process to combine. Pour the mixture over the blintzes.

3. Place a stainless-steel trivet into the pressure cooker cooking pot and add the 1½ cups (350 ml) water to the pot. Using a foil sling or other type of sling, lower the casserole dish onto the trivet.

4. Lock the lid and close the pressure valve. Cook for 30 minutes on High Pressure. When the beep sounds, allow a full natural pressure release.

5. Brown the blintzes under the broiler, if desired, before serving.

6. Warm the Berry Compote and serve with the blintzes.

🤍 TOG TIP!

If desired, cut the blintzes into thirds, combine them with the soufflé mixture, and then pour everything into the casserole dish to cook in the pressure cooker. Cut blintzes are easier to serve in a buffet-like situation.

Passover Vegetable Matzo Lasagna

PREP: 20 MIN.
COOK: 12 MIN.
YIELD: 4 SERVINGS

When you want lasagna during Passover, this dish is a perfect dairy meal.

Mushroom Mince

1 tablespoon salted butter (14 g) or
 extra-virgin olive oil (15 ml)
8 ounces (225 g) cremini mushrooms
2 tablespoons (30 ml) Worcestershire
 sauce (see TOG Tip!)
2 tablespoons (30 ml) Shaoxing wine or
 dry sherry
1 medium zucchini, chopped

Cheese Filling

1 cup cottage cheese (225 g) or ricotta
 cheese (250 g)
½ cup (50 g) grated Parmesan cheese
2 large eggs
2 tablespoons (8 g) fresh flat-leaf parsley
 leaves, minced
1 teaspoon sea salt

Lasagna

3 sheets matzo
16 ounces (454 g) shredded mozzarella
 cheese
3 cups (750 g) pasta sauce, divided
¼ cup (25 g) grated Parmesan cheese,
 plus more for garnishing (optional)
1½ cups (360 ml) water, for the
 cooking pot

1. **To make the mushroom mince:** In a large skillet over medium heat, melt the butter. Add the mushrooms, Worcestershire sauce, and wine. Sauté for 5 minutes.

2. Transfer the mixture to a food processor, then process for 10 seconds. Add the chopped zucchini and process for 5 seconds more, until chunky.

3. **To make the cheese filling:** In a medium bowl, combine all the filling ingredients.

4. **To make the lasagna:** In a 5½-inch-square (14 cm) pan, place 1 matzo sheet. Spread one-third of the cheese filling over it. Sprinkle on 4 ounces (115 g) of the mozzarella cheese and one-third of the mushroom mince. Top with ½ cup (125 g) of the pasta sauce. Repeat the layering 2 more times. Sprinkle the top with Parmesan cheese and the remaining 4 ounces (115 g) mozzarella cheese.

5. Place a stainless-steel trivet into the pressure cooker cooking pot and add the water to the pot. Place the lasagna on the trivet.

6. Lock the lid and close the pressure valve. Cook for 12 minutes on High Pressure. When the beep sounds, wait 5 minutes, then release the remaining pressure.

7. Remove the lasagna, slice, and serve. Serve with the remaining 1½ cups (375 g) pasta sauce and more Parmesan cheese, if desired.

💟 **TOG TIP!**

For a vegetarian version, omit the Worcestershire sauce.

Tzimmes
(Sweet Root Vegetable and Fruit Stew)

PREP: 20 MIN.
COOK: 3 MIN.
YIELD: 4–6 SERVINGS

This stew, traditionally served at Rosh Hashanah and Passover, is good any time of the year. *Tzimmes* means "make a big fuss," but this recipe is hardly a fuss. A piece of flanken or brisket is sometimes added for flavor. Tzimmes can be made the day before and tastes even better the next day.

1 pound (454 g) carrots, peeled and cut into 1½-inch (3.5 cm) chunks
1 cup (175 g) dried pitted prunes
1 cup (130 g) dried apricots
¼ cup (35 g) raisins
2 pounds (907 g) sweet potatoes (or yams), peeled and cut into 2-inch (5 cm) chunks
1 cup (240 ml) orange juice
¼ cup (80 g) honey, or to taste
2 tablespoons (30 g) packed light brown sugar, or more to taste
1 teaspoon kosher salt
1 teaspoon ground cinnamon
⅛ teaspoon freshly grated nutmeg
2 tablespoons (28 g) salted butter (see TOG Tips!)
¼ cup (25 g) walnuts, chopped
2 teaspoons grated orange zest

1. In the pressure cooker cooking pot, place (in this order) the carrots, prunes, apricots, raisins, and sweet potatoes.

2. In a small bowl, whisk together the orange juice, honey, brown sugar, kosher salt, cinnamon, and nutmeg, and pour the mixture into the cooking pot. Dot the top with the butter.

3. Lock the lid and close the pressure valve. Cook for 3 minutes on High Pressure. When the beep sounds, wait 3 minutes, then release the remaining pressure.

4. Remove the lid, and if desired, select Sauté or Browning and simmer the mixture to thicken.

5. Transfer to a serving bowl and garnish with chopped walnuts and orange zest.

🩶 TOG TIPS!

For flavor variations, add 1 to 2 teaspoons minced fresh ginger or ¼ teaspoon ground ginger; cranberries instead of raisins; pineapple juice instead of orange juice; or cherries, pineapple, and/or coconut flakes. Make it savory with ¼ cup (40 g) sliced onions.

For a dairy meal, omit the butter.

Tzimmes can be placed under the broiler to crisp, if desired.

Gefilte Fish
(Jewish Fish Balls)

PREP: 30 MIN.
COOK: 30 MIN.
YIELD: 12 BALLS

A favorite and popular appetizer for the Passover Seder, gefilte fish are basically balls of fish cooked in a rich fish broth.

Fish Stock

Fish trimmings, including head, bones, and skin (see TOG Tips!)
2 medium onions, unpeeled
2 teaspoons kosher salt, divided
2 teaspoons sugar, divided
¼ teaspoon ground white pepper
3 quarts (2.8 L) water

Gefilte Fish Balls

4 large carrots, peeled, divided
1 medium onion, peeled
3 large egg whites
1 teaspoon kosher salt
¼ teaspoon ground white pepper
2 teaspoons sugar
½ cup (60 g) matzo meal (or 3 pieces of matzo)
4 pounds (1.8 kg) whole fish, such as whitefish, pike, or cod, trimmed with trimmings reserved (see TOG Tips!)

🩶 TOG TIPS!

Ask your fishmonger to clean and grind the fish for you, reserving all the trimmings, including the head, bones, and skin.

Depending on the fish type, you may need 2 whole fish to equal 4 pounds (1.8 kg).

Serve on a lettuce leaf with a carrot slice on top. Add a dollop of horseradish or beet horseradish.

1. **To make the fish stock:** In the pressure cooker cooking pot, combine the fish trimmings, onions, 1 teaspoon of the salt, 1 teaspoon of the sugar, white pepper, and water.

2. Lock the lid and close the pressure valve. Cook for 15 minutes on High Pressure. When the beep sounds, allow a full natural pressure release.

3. **To make the gefilte fish balls:** While the stock cooks, in a food processor, combine 1 carrot, the onion, egg whites, salt, white pepper, sugar, and matzo meal. Process until the carrot and onion are minced. Add the fish and pulse just until the mixture is combined. Transfer to a bowl and refrigerate.

4. When all the pressure has released, remove the lid and strain the stock through a fine-mesh strainer into a bowl and discard the solids. Rinse out the cooking pot and add the strained broth back into the pot. Select Low Pressure and 15 minutes on the pressure cooker. Add the remaining 1 teaspoon each kosher salt and sugar.

5. Remove the gefilte fish ball mixture from the refrigerator and form the mixture into 12 egg-shaped balls. Use a large spoon to gently place the fish balls into the hot liquid.

6. Slice the remaining 3 carrots and add them to the cooking pot. Lock the lid and close the pressure valve. Time has already been set. When the beep sounds, allow a full natural pressure release.

7. Remove the lid and use a slotted spoon to transfer the fish balls and carrots to a container and let cool for 20 minutes.

8. Strain the stock through a fine-mesh strainer and pour over the gefilte fish. Refrigerate until chilled (see TOG Tips!).

Grandma Rose's Luchen Kugel
(Jewish Noodle Pudding)

PREP: 10 MIN.
COOK: 22 MIN.
YIELD: 8 SERVINGS

Kugel is a favorite Jewish holiday dish. I have shared this recipe, my grandma's, throughout the years, so please enjoy. Try using fun-shaped pasta, or colored pasta or noodles.

Noodles
8 ounces (225 g) wide egg noodles

Filling
3 large eggs
8 ounces (227 g) cottage cheese
4 ounces (113 g) sour cream
½ cup (50 g) sugar
½ teaspoon freshly squeezed lemon juice
½ teaspoon kosher salt
⅛ teaspoon ground cinnamon
½ cup (75 g) raisins, soaked in water for 15 minutes (see TOG Tips!)
1 tablespoon salted butter, divided
1½ cups (360 ml) water, for the cooking pot

Topping (see TOG Tips!)
¼ cup (7 g) corn flakes, crushed
1 teaspoon sugar
¼ teaspoon ground cinnamon

♥ TOG TIPS!
Dried diced mixed fruit can be substituted for the raisins.

I rarely use the topping myself, but I do like to put the kugel under the broiler to crisp the top.

For a 7-inch (18 cm) pan, cook for 19 minutes; for an 8-inch (20 cm) pan, double the recipe and cook for 30 minutes.

1. **To make the noodles:** In your pressure cooker cooking pot, combine the egg noodles with enough water to just barely cover them. Lock the lid and close the pressure valve. Cook for 0 minutes on High Pressure. When the beep sounds, toggle the pressure valve to quickly release all the pressure.

2. Remove the lid and drain the noodles in a colander, running them under cool water to stop the cooking.

3. **To make the filling:** In a large bowl, beat the eggs well. Add the cottage cheese, sour cream, sugar, lemon juice, kosher salt, and cinnamon to the beaten eggs. Mix thoroughly to combine.

4. Drain the raisins and fold them into the filling. Add the noodles and gently fold to combine.

5. Grease a 1½-quart (1.4 L) casserole dish with 1½ teaspoons of the butter (See TOG Tips!). Pour the noodles into the pan. Dot the kugel with the remaining 1½ teaspoons butter. Cover the pan with a lid or aluminum foil.

6. Place a stainless-steel trivet into the pressure cooker cooking pot and add the water to the pot. Using a foil sling, lower the pan onto the trivet. Lock the lid and close the pressure valve. Cook for 22 minutes on High Pressure. When the beep sounds, wait 10 minutes, then release the remaining pressure.

7. **To make the topping:** In a small bowl, combine all the topping ingredients. Sprinkle it over the kugel. Dot with the remaining 1½ teaspoons of butter and place it under the broiler for a few minutes.

Matzo Ball Soup (Chicken Soup)

Every Jewish kid grows up with a chicken soup recipe that was handed down by their grandma. It's what we eat when we are happy, when we are sad, and when we are sick. Jewish Penicillin is what it is often called. The chicken soup can stand alone and is not quite traditional, as I flavor it with a little oregano. Whether you love matzo ball "floaters" or "sinkers," my easy recipe yields beautiful and fluffy matzo balls that can be made in advance and pair perfectly with the soup.

PREP: 1 HR.
COOK: 85 MIN.
YIELD: 8 SERVINGS

Chicken Soup

1 whole chicken hen (about 5 pounds, or 2.3 kg), breast meat and skin removed and reserved
2 pounds (907 g) chicken backs
½ cup (120 ml) water
1 bunch celery, leaves, stalks, and base separated
1 large onion, unpeeled and halved
¼ cup (15 g) flat-leaf parsley leaves
2 garlic cloves
1 teaspoon peppercorns
1 bay leaf
2 tablespoons (37 g) kosher salt, plus more as needed
½ teaspoon freshly ground black pepper, plus more as needed
3 to 6 quarts (2.8 to 5.6 L) water (depending on the size of your pressure cooker)
1 cup (120 g) diced celery
2 to 3 carrots, sliced
2 teaspoons dried oregano
1 Matzo Ball recipe, "floaters" or "sinkers" (optional; recipe follows)

Matzo Ball Mixture: "Floaters" or "Sinkers"

1 cup (120 g) matzo meal
1 teaspoon salt
3 large eggs
¼ cup (60 ml) schmaltz (chicken fat)
For floaters: ¼ cup (60 ml) seltzer water (or ½ teaspoon baking soda combined with ¼ cup, (60 ml), water)
For sinkers: 1¼ cups (60 ml) water

Matzo Ball Cooking Liquid

4 quarts (3.8 L) water
2 tablespoons (37 g) kosher salt
½ teaspoon freshly ground black pepper (optional)
2 celery stalks, chopped
¼ teaspoon dried dill weed (optional)

1. **To make the chicken soup:** Remove the breast meat from the bones, reserving the bones. Thinly slice the breast meat and refrigerate until needed.

2. On your pressure cooker, select Sauté or Browning and fully heat the cooking pot.

3. Place the reserved chicken skin with fat into the cooking pot. Cook for 5 minutes without stirring. Transfer ¼ cup (60 ml) rendered chicken fat ("schmaltz") to a small bowl and set aside for the matzo balls. Leave the skin in the pot.

♥ **TOG TIPS!**

The chicken soup can be made in advance and refrigerated. Browning the chicken skin will add a richness and depth, along with a glossy golden broth. So don't skim off all the fat; embrace the fat.

Make sure not to overwork the matzo balls. Combine the ingredients until they just come together and be gentle when forming into balls.

4. Pour in the ½ cup (120 ml water) and deglaze the cooking pot, scraping up any browned bits from the bottom of the pot. Turn off the pressure cooker.

5. To the cooking pot, add the celery leaves, celery base, onion, parsley, garlic, peppercorns, bay leaf, kosher salt, black pepper, and the remaining chicken pieces, and chicken backs. Cover with water to the cooking pot's fill line.

6. Lock the lid and close the pressure valve. Cook for 75 minutes on High Pressure.

7. When the beep sounds, wait 20 minutes, then carefully release the remaining pressure. Remove the lid. Strain the broth through a fine-mesh strainer and discard all the solids. Excess fat will rise to the top. Place a paper towel on top of the soup to absorb the fat. Quickly remove the paper towel and discard it. Set the broth aside and cook the matzo balls.

8. Return the concentrated, strained chicken broth to the cooking pot and add a few cups of water as necessary. Season with more salt and pepper if necessary.

9. Add the diced celery, sliced carrots, oregano, and the reserved chicken breast slices. Select Sauté or Browning and simmer for 5 to 10 minutes, or until the carrots are tender. Eat the soup by itself or add matzo balls.

1. **To make the matzo ball mixture:** In a medium bowl, combine the matzo meal and salt. In another bowl, whisk together the eggs, schmaltz, and seltzer water (for floaters) or water (for sinkers). Gently fold the dry ingredients into the wet ingredients. Do not overmix; combine the ingredients just until they come together. Cover with plastic wrap and refrigerate for at least 1 hour.

2. **To make the cooking liquid for the matzo balls:** On your pressure cooker, select Low Pressure and 30 minutes. Combine the water, salt, black pepper (if using), and celery in the cooking pot.

3. Remove the matzo ball mixture from the refrigerator and gently form it into 1½-inch (4 cm) balls and place them on a plate. The matzo balls will expand as they cook.

4. When the cooking liquid begins to simmer, use a slotted spoon to carefully place the matzo balls, one at a time, into the cooking liquid.

5. Lock the lid and close the pressure valve. Cook for 10 minutes on Low Pressure. When the beep sounds, wait 15 minutes, then slowly release the remaining pressure by toggling the pressure valve to release a little pressure at a time. Releasing the pressure too fast will cause the matzo balls to break.

6. Remove the lid and transfer the matzo balls to a plate (do not store them in liquid). The matzo balls should be light and fluffy. If they are hard in the center, you may need to cook them longer. Discard the cooking liquid and solids. For smaller pressure cookers, cook the matzo balls in 2 batches.

7. **To assemble the bowls:** Place 1 or 2 matzo balls in each bowl and ladle in the chicken soup. Garnish with dill, if desired.

Jewish-Style Sweet-and-Sour Stuffed Cabbage

PREP: 45 MIN.
COOK: 9 MIN.
YIELD: 6 SERVINGS

My grandma would be so proud of this stuffed cabbage recipe. Sweet-and-sour stuffed cabbage, also called *holishkes*, has been a staple of Eastern European Jews since the fourteenth century. Ashkenazi Jews everywhere have their own special recipes and traditions.

Stuffed Cabbage

1 cup (240 ml) water, for the cooking pot
1 large head green cabbage
1½ pounds (680 g) ground beef
1 large egg
½ cup (93 g) long-grain white rice (see TOG Tips!)
¼ cup (40 g) grated onion plus 2 large onions, sliced, divided
1 garlic clove, minced
1 teaspoon kosher salt
½ teaspoon freshly ground black pepper

Sauce

23 ounces (680 ml) tomato juice, reserving 1 cup (240 ml), divided
1 can (15 ounces, or 425 g) tomato sauce
¼ cup (60 g) packed light brown sugar
Juice of 2 large lemons
1 garlic clove, minced
1 tablespoon coconut oil (15 ml), vegetable shortening (14 g), or vegetable oil (15 ml)
2 teaspoons kosher salt
½ teaspoon freshly ground black pepper
1 can (28 ounces, or 794 g) whole tomatoes in puree or tomato puree

1. **To make the stuffed cabbage:** Add the water to the pressure cooker cooking pot. Place the cabbage on the trivet in the pot. Lock the lid and close the pressure valve. Cook for 1 minute on High Pressure. When the beep sounds, wait 5 minutes, then release the remaining pressure.

2. Remove the lid and transfer the cabbage to a colander. Run it under cold water to cool. Dump out the water from the cooking pot and rinse the pot. Place the pot back into the pressure cooker.

3. Remove the cabbage's core. Carefully remove 14 to 20 leaves. Carefully shave off the thick part of the vein at the base of each leaf. Set the leaves aside. Chop the remaining cabbage and set aside.

4. In a large bowl, combine the beef, egg, rice, grated onion, garlic, kosher salt, and black pepper. Combine well. Set aside.

5. **To make the sauce:** In a heavy-duty blender or regular blender, combine 15 ounces (440 ml) of the tomato juice, the tomato sauce, brown sugar, lemon juice, garlic, coconut oil, salt, and black pepper. Process to combine. Add the whole tomatoes and process just to crush. You want some texture in the sauce.

6. Working with one cabbage leaf at a time, place a small handful of the meat mixture at the base of the leaf. Fold in the sides and roll up the leaf, tucking in the sides as you go. Repeat until all filling has been used.

7. Place one-third of the chopped cabbage and sliced onions into the bottom of the pressure cooker cooking pot. Pour in the remaining 1 cup (240 ml) of tomato juice (see TOG Tips!). Place a short-legged stainless-steel trivet into pressure cooker cooking pot over the cabbage layer. Place half the cabbage rolls on the trivet. Add half the remaining cabbage and onion over the top, and cover with half the sauce. Add another layer of cabbage rolls, top with the remaining cabbage and onion, and cover with the remaining sauce.

8. Lock the lid and close the pressure valve. Cook for 9 minutes on High Pressure. When the beep sounds, wait 15 to 20 minutes, then release the remaining pressure.

9. Remove the lid and use a slotted spoon to transfer the cabbage rolls to a plate and pour over the sauce to serve.

♥ **TOG TIPS!**

If using brown rice, add the raw rice to the pressure cooker cooking pot when you precook the cabbage. After the pressure is released, strain out the excess water from the rice and then add the brown rice to the meat mixture.

The reason 1 cup (240 ml) of the tomato juice is reserved for the buffer layer is to keep the sugar directly off the bottom of the cooking pot.

Some people top the dish with raisins or crushed gingersnaps, or even add candied ginger to the sauce.

Notes

PASTA AND ITALIAN FAVORITES

SPAGHETTI WITH HOMEMADE SAUCE

Chicken Marsala

BEEF AND MACARONI

WILD MUSHROOM RISOTTO

ITALIAN MEATBALLS IN RED WINE SAUCE

CHICKEN PICCATA

BACON BUTTERNUT PASTA

SPAGHETTI SQUASH & MEAT SAUCE

and *Penne alla Vodka*

Spaghetti with Homemade Sauce

PREP: 10 MIN.
COOK: 5 MIN.
YIELD: 4 SERVINGS

Dinner on the fly, no problem! This easy spaghetti dinner will taste like you have been simmering the sauce all day. Only you will know that it took 30 minutes! For just a spaghetti sauce recipe, see page 11.

2 tablespoons (15 ml) extra-virgin olive oil
½ large onion, chopped
2 garlic cloves, minced
1 can (28 ounces, or 794 g) diced tomatoes
2½ cups (600 ml) chicken stock or broth (or water)
1 can (15 ounces, 425 g) tomato sauce
3 ounces (85 g) tomato paste
¼ cup (60 ml) red wine (a good Cabernet)
2 teaspoons dried basil
2 teaspoons dried parsley flakes
1 teaspoon dried oregano
1 teaspoon packed light brown sugar
1 teaspoon sea salt
1 teaspoon fennel seeds, crushed
¼ teaspoon Sambal Oelek Ground Fresh Chili Paste or red pepper flakes
¼ teaspoon freshly ground black pepper
Parmesan cheese rind
1 pound (454 g) good-quality spaghetti broken in half (see TOG Tips!)

1. On your pressure cooker, select Sauté or Browning and fully heat the cooking pot.

2. Add the olive oil, followed by the onion, to the cooking pot. Sauté for 2 minutes.

3. Add the garlic and sauté for 30 seconds more. Add the remaining ingredients, except for the spaghetti, and mix well. Add the spaghetti and lightly push it into the sauce.

4. Lock the lid and close the pressure valve. Cook for 5 minutes on High Pressure. When the beep sounds, wait 5 minutes, then carefully jiggle the pressure valve to release the remaining pressure.

5. Remove the lid and break apart any pasta that is stuck together. If the pasta is too firm for your liking, stir everything together, separating any stuck pasta, and replace the lid. The residual heat will continue to cook the pasta to desired doneness. Serve (see TOG Tips!).

♥ TOG TIPS!
Serve with a dollop of ricotta cheese, a shaving of fresh Parmesan or Asiago cheese, and a garnish of fresh parsley, if you like.

Chicken Marsala

This restaurant-quality meal is perfect for a dinner party. For a different take on the dish, try the soup version (page 102).

PREP: 30 MIN.
COOK: 2 MIN.
YIELD: 4 SERVINGS

2 boneless, skinless chicken breasts, butterflied
¼ cup (45 g) potato starch
1 tablespoon (15 ml) kosher salt
½ teaspoon freshly ground black pepper
3 tablespoons (45 ml) extra-virgin olive oil
3 ounces (85 g) prosciutto, diced
1 cup (240 ml) dry Marsala wine, divided (see TOG Tip!)
2 tablespoons (28 g) salted butter
1 pound (454 g) cremini mushrooms or wild mushrooms, sliced
2 large shallots or 1 small onion, sliced
3 garlic cloves, minced
½ cup (120 ml) chicken stock or broth
½ teaspoon herbes de Provence
3 fresh thyme sprigs
Fresh flat-leaf parsley leaves, for garnishing

💜 **TOG TIP!**
Use a good, dry Marsala wine, one that you would enjoy drinking. Marsala wine labeled "cooking" is not recommended.

1. Place each piece of chicken between plastic wrap or waxed paper and lightly pound until thin and even.

2. In a shallow dish, combine the potato starch, kosher salt, and black pepper. Dredge the chicken through the seasoned potato starch and shake off the excess starch.

3. Line a plate with paper towels and set aside. On your pressure cooker, select Sauté or Browning, adjust the heat to High, and fully heat the cooking pot.

4. Add the olive oil to the cooking pot. Working in batches, brown the chicken cutlets for about 10 seconds per side to sear. Transfer the cutlets to the paper towel–lined plate.

5. Adjust the pressure cooker setting to Normal and add the prosciutto. Pour in ¼ cup (60 ml) of the Marsala and deglaze the cooking pot, scraping up any browned bits from the bottom of the pot. Continue to cook the prosciutto to render its fat.

6. When the liquid reduces and the prosciutto begins to brown, add the butter to melt.

7. Add ¼ cup (60 ml) of the Marsala, the mushrooms, and onion. Sauté for about 3 minutes, until the onion is soft and the liquid is syrupy.

8. Stir in the garlic and pour in the remaining ½ cup (120 ml) Marsala. Let bubble for about 2 minutes to reduce slightly. Turn off the pressure cooker and stir in the chicken stock, herbes de Provence, and thyme. Return the chicken to the pot.

9. Lock the lid and close the pressure valve. Cook for 2 minutes on High Pressure. When the beep sounds, wait 5 minutes, then release the remaining pressure.

10. Remove the lid, then remove and discard the thyme. Plate and serve garnished with parsley.

Beef and Macaroni

Beef and macaroni has so many names. Bolognese and Johnny Marzetti are just a couple of them. Any way you call this recipe, you are going to love the homemade meat sauce. Your family and friends will think you were cooking all day.

1 tablespoon (15 ml) extra-virgin olive oil
1 pound (454 g) ground beef (see TOG Tips!)
½ onion, finely diced
½ green bell pepper, diced
3 garlic cloves, minced
16 ounces (454 g) hearty pasta (such as cavatappi; see TOG Tips!)
2½ cups (600 ml) water
1 can (28 ounces, or 794 g) tomato puree
1 can (15 ounces, or 425 g) tomato sauce
3 ounces (85 g) tomato paste
¼ cup (60 ml) dry red wine (a good Cabernet)
1 tablespoon (15 ml) Worcestershire sauce
2 teaspoons dried basil
2 teaspoons dried parsley flakes
2 teaspoons sea salt
1 teaspoon packed light brown sugar
¼ teaspoon red pepper flakes
¼ teaspoon freshly ground black pepper
Freshly grated Parmesan cheese, for topping

1. On your pressure cooker, select Sauté or Browning and fully heat the cooking pot.

2. Add the olive oil to the cooking pot and then the beef. Cook until partially browned, breaking it up with a spoon as you cook.

3. Add the onion and green bell pepper. Sauté for 2 minutes, until the meat is mostly brown.

4. Add the garlic and sauté for 1 minute more. Drain the pot of excess grease, if needed.

5. Stir in all the remaining ingredients.

6. Lock the lid and close the pressure valve. Cook for 5 minutes on High Pressure. When the beep sounds, wait 5 minutes, then carefully toggle the pressure valve back and forth to slowly release the pressure.

7. Serve with the Parmesan cheese for topping.

🩶 TOG TIPS!

If using ground turkey or chicken instead of beef, add another tablespoon (15 ml) of Worcestershire sauce.

Check the pasta package for the recommended cooking time. My rule of thumb is to cook the pasta for half of the shorter cooking time indicated on the package and subtract 2 minutes. Error on the side of less time, as you can always simmer further after the pressure is released.

Wild Mushroom Risotto

PREP: 10 MIN.
COOK: 4 MIN.
YIELD: 6 SERVINGS

Your taste buds will dance with glee after one bite of this risotto, and your hands will thank you for not having to stir, stir, stir. As an aside, this was the first stove-top recipe I ever converted for an electric pressure cooker.

4 ounces (115 g) dried wild mushrooms or 8 ounces (225 g) fresh mushrooms (see TOG Tip!)

1 tablespoon (14 g) salted butter

1 tablespoon (15 ml) extra-virgin olive oil

1½ cups (9 ounces, or 255 g) Arborio rice

3 large shallots, chopped

1 teaspoon fennel seeds, crushed

½ cup (120 ml) dry white wine

2 cups (480 ml) chicken or vegetable broth

1½ cups (350 ml) mushroom soaking water (see step 1) or fresh water

½ teaspoon sea salt

1 cup (3 ounces, or 85 g) Asiago cheese, shredded

2 tablespoons (8 g) fresh flat-leaf parsley leaves, chopped

Freshly ground black pepper, to taste

♥ TOG TIP!

For fresh mushrooms, use cremini; white button mushrooms are not recommended for this dish.

1. If using dried mushrooms, in a medium bowl, combine them with 2 cups (75 ml) boiling water. Let soak for 10 minutes to soften. Using a slotted spoon, transfer the mushrooms to a cutting board and coarsely chop. Reserve 1½ cups (350 ml) of the soaking liquid. If using fresh mushrooms, clean and slice them.

2. On your pressure cooker, select Sauté or Browning and fully heat the cooking pot.

3. Add the butter and olive oil to the cooking pot.

4. Add the rice, shallots, and fennel seeds. Sauté for 3 minutes, stirring.

5. Add the white wine and sauté for about 1 minute more, until almost evaporated, stirring frequently.

6. Stir in the chicken broth, the 1½ cups (350 ml) reserved mushroom soaking water or fresh water (if using fresh mushrooms), sea salt, and mushrooms.

7. Lock the lid and close the pressure valve. Cook for 4 minutes on High Pressure. When the beep sounds, carefully toggle the pressure valve back and forth to slowly release the pressure. Turn off the pressure cooker.

8. Select Sauté or Browning. Remove the lid and stir the rice for about 2 minutes, until creamy and tender but still firm to the bite. If more liquid is needed, stir in more broth or reserved soaking liquid, a little at a time, until desired creaminess is achieved.

9. Stir in the cheese and parsley, and season with black pepper.

Italian Meatballs in Red Wine Sauce

PREP: 25 MIN.
COOK: 10 MIN.
YIELD: 12 MEATBALLS

The layers of flavors in these meatballs go on and on and on. The tender meatballs are first seared and then simmered in a red wine marinara that even the most sophisticated palates will enjoy.

Meatball Seasoning

7 ounces (7 g) dry-packed sun-dried tomatoes (See TOG Tips!)
5 ounces (115 g) ricotta cheese
1 cup (95 g) old-fashioned rolled oats (not instant)
¼ cup (15 g) fresh flat-leaf parsley leaves, plus more for garnishing
3 tablespoons (19 g) Parmesan cheese, freshly shredded, plus more for garnishing
3 tablespoons (45 ml) heavy cream
2 garlic cloves
1 large egg
1¼ teaspoons dried oregano
1 teaspoon kosher salt
1 teaspoon fennel seeds
1 teaspoon red pepper flakes
½ teaspoon smoked paprika
½ teaspoon ground allspice
½ teaspoon ground cumin
½ teaspoon freshly ground black pepper, plus more as needed

Meatballs

1 pound (454 g) ground beef
8 ounces (225 g) ground pork
3 tablespoons (34 g) potato starch (see TOG Tips!)
2 tablespoons (30 ml) extra-virgin olive oil, plus more as needed

Sauce

1 tablespoon (15 ml) extra-virgin olive oil
1 small onion, finely diced
½ medium carrot, peeled and minced
2 garlic cloves, minced
1¼ cups (300 ml) dry red wine
1 tablespoon (16 g) tomato paste
½ cup (120 ml) beef stock
1 can (28 ounces, or 794 g) tomato puree or crushed tomatoes
¾ teaspoon dried oregano
2 fresh basil sprigs, plus more for garnishing

💙 TOG TIPS!

If you are intolerant to sun-dried tomatoes, omit them and the paprika and use 2 ounces (55 g) prosciutto instead.

Searing the meatballs after dredging in potato starch prevents them from sticking to the cooking pot.

1. **To make the meatball seasoning:** In a food processor, combine all the meatball seasoning ingredients and process until well combined.

2. **To make the meatballs:** Add the beef and pork to the meatball seasoning and pulse to combine. Form the meat mixture into 12 meatballs. Place the potato starch in a shallow bowl and dredge the meatballs through the starch (see TOG Tips!).

3. On your pressure cooker, select Sauté or Browning and fully heat the cooking pot.

4. Add the olive oil to the cooking pot.

5. Working in batches, sear the meatballs for 1 to 2 minutes, until slightly crisp. Allow the meatballs to brown untouched. Once a crust forms, use a spatula to easily roll them to the next side. If needed, add more olive oil to the pot. Transfer the meatballs to a plate.

6. Pour in ¼ cup (60 ml) of water and deglaze the cooking pot, scraping up any browned bits from the bottom of the pot. Quickly dump out the water and bits and start with a clean pot. Do not turn off the pressure cooker.

7. **To make the sauce:** In the cooking pot, combine the olive oil, onion, and carrot. Sauté for 2 minutes.

8. Add the garlic and sauté for 30 seconds more.

9. Pour in the red wine and deglaze the cooking pot, scraping up any browned bits from the bottom of the pot.

10. Stir in the tomato paste and simmer for about 5 minutes to reduce the wine.

11. Stir in the beef stock, tomato puree, oregano, and basil, making sure nothing is stuck to the bottom of the pot.

12. Carefully add the meatballs to the sauce.

13. Lock the lid and close the pressure valve. Cook for 10 minutes on Low Pressure. When the beep sounds, wait 15 minutes, then release the remaining pressure.

14. Season with black pepper and serve garnished with Parmesan cheese, basil, and parsley.

Chicken Piccata

Chicken piccata is an Italian favorite. It is basically pan-fried chicken schnitzel with a simple-to-make lemon cream sauce.

PREP: 15 MIN.
COOK: 2 MIN.
YIELD: 4 SERVINGS

2 boneless, skinless chicken breasts, butterflied

1 teaspoon sea salt

¼ teaspoon freshly ground black pepper

¼ cup (45 g) potato starch

6 tablespoons (85 g) salted butter, divided

3 tablespoons (45 ml) extra-virgin olive oil, divided

1 large shallot, minced

½ cup (120 ml) chicken stock or broth

⅓ cup (80 ml) dry white wine or more chicken stock

3 large lemons, 2 thinly sliced and 1 juiced, divided

3 tablespoons (26 g) whole capers, drained and rinsed

⅓ cup (20 g) fresh flat-leaf parsley leaves, chopped

♥ TOG TIP!

If you like a thicker sauce, make a slurry: Transfer ¼ cup (60 ml) sauce from the pot to a small bowl. Add 2 teaspoons potato starch to it and whisk until smooth. Add the slurry back to the cooking pot and whisk to combine.

1. Place the chicken pieces between sheets of waxed paper and lightly pound the thicker parts to match the thinner sides. Season with the sea salt and black pepper. Place the potato starch in a shallow bowl and dredge the chicken through the potato starch.

2. On your pressure cooker, select Sauté or Browning and adjust the heat to High. Let the cooking pot fully heat.

3. Add 2 tablespoons (28 g) of the butter and 2 tablespoons (30 ml) of the olive oil to the cooking pot. When the butter melts, add half the chicken and sear for about 1 minute on each side, until brown. Transfer the chicken to a clean plate. Add the remaining tablespoon (15 ml) olive oil and 2 tablespoons (28 g) of the butter. When the butter melts, add the remaining chicken. Sear for about 1 minute on each side, until brown. Transfer to a plate.

4. Add the shallot and sauté until slightly brown, being careful not to burn. Pour in the chicken stock and white wine, and deglaze the cooking pot, scraping up any browned bits from the bottom of the pot. Add the lemon slices from 2 lemons and return the chicken to the cooking pot.

5. Lock the lid and close the pressure valve. Cook for 2 minutes on High Pressure. When the beep sounds, wait 5 minutes, then release the remaining pressure. Turn off the pressure cooker.

6. Remove the lid and transfer the chicken and lemon slices to an oven-safe serving plate. (The lemon will become bitter if not removed.) Place it in an oven on low heat or cover to keep warm.

7. On your pressure cooker, select Sauté or Browning. Add the remaining 2 tablespoons (28 g) butter to the sauce in the cooking pot and whisk to thicken (see TOG Tip!). Turn off the pressure cooker.

8. Stir in the capers, lemon juice from the remaining lemon, and parsley. Spoon the sauce over the chicken and serve.

Bacon Butternut Pasta

PREP: 20 MIN.
COOK: 4 MIN.
YIELD: 6 SERVINGS

Butternut squash becomes the sauce in this pasta recipe. This dish is savory yet slightly sweet, with complex levels of flavor that are sure to please any pasta lover.

6 bacon slices, cut into 2-inch (5 cm) pieces
1 teaspoon extra-virgin olive oil
1 tablespoon (14 g) salted butter
1 small onion, chopped
2 garlic cloves, minced
3½ cups (28 ounces, or 820 ml) chicken broth
1 teaspoon kosher salt
¼ teaspoon freshly ground pepper
1½ pounds (680 g) butternut squash, chopped into 1-inch (2.5 cm) pieces
16 ounces (454 g) penne pasta (see TOG Tip!)
3 cups (90 g) fresh spinach, roughly chopped
Freshly grated Asiago cheese, for garnishing

1. On your pressure cooker, select Sauté or Browning and fully heat the cooking pot.

2. Add the bacon to the cooking pot and sauté until crisp. Remove the bacon from the pot and drain, leaving the grease in the pot.

3. Add the olive oil, butter, and onion. Sauté until the onion is translucent.

4. Add the garlic and sauté for 1 minute. Add the chicken broth and deglaze the cooking pot, scraping up any browned bits from the bottom of the pot.

5. Add the bacon, kosher salt, black pepper, butternut squash, and pasta.

6. Lock the lid and close the pressure value. Cook for 4 minutes on High Pressure. When the beep sounds, wait 5 minutes, then release the remaining pressure.

7. Remove the lid and toss in the spinach. Stir to combine.

8. Plate the dish and garnish with the cheese.

♥ TOG TIP!

This dish can be made with low-carb or gluten-free pasta. Use the shortest cooking time on the package of pasta and subtract 2 minutes.

Spaghetti Squash and Meat Sauce

PREP: 20 MIN.
COOK: 10–14 MIN.
YIELD: 4 SERVINGS

This dish prepared in one pot will change your life. Enjoy a healthy low-carb, low-fat, low-calorie "spaghetti" and meat sauce dinner!

2 tablespoons (30 ml) extra-virgin olive oil

1 pound (454 g) ground beef or turkey

¼ cup (40 g) onion, diced

1 celery rib, diced

2 garlic cloves, minced

¾ cup (180 ml) beef broth

½ cup (120 ml) red wine (Cabernet) or more beef broth

6 ounces (170 g) mushrooms, sliced (optional)

1 can (28 ounces, or 794 g) crushed tomatoes with puree

1 can (15 ounces, or 425 g) tomato sauce

1 can (6 ounces, or 170 g) tomato paste, divided

2 tablespoons (30 ml) Worcestershire sauce

2 teaspoons dried basil

1 teaspoon dried oregano

2 teaspoons dried parsley flakes

2 teaspoons sugar

1 teaspoon sea salt, or to taste

¼ teaspoon freshly ground black pepper, or to taste

1 rind (1 inch, or 2.5 cm) Parmesan cheese

2 bay leaves

1 spaghetti squash (2 to 4 pounds, or 908 g to 1.8 kg), scrubbed and stem end trimmed

1 tablespoon (15 ml) fish sauce

1. On your pressure cooker, select Sauté or Browning and fully heat the cooking pot.

2. Add the olive oil to the cooking pot, then add the ground beef, onion, and celery. Sauté for about 3 minutes, until the ingredients begin to caramelize. Pour out any excess grease. Add the garlic and sauté for 1 minute more.

3. Pour in the beef broth and red wine and deglaze the cooking pot, scraping up any browned bits from the bottom of the pot.

4. Stir in the mushrooms (if using), crushed tomatoes, tomato sauce, half the tomato paste, the Worcestershire sauce, basil, oregano, parsley, sugar, sea salt, and black pepper. Mix well. Push the cheese rind and bay leaves into the sauce.

5. Place the whole spaghetti squash in the pot on top of the sauce, pushing it down into the sauce, if needed.

6. Lock the lid and close the pressure valve. Cook for 10 to 14 minutes, depending on the size of the squash, on High Pressure. When the beep sounds, allow a full natural pressure release.

7. Remove the lid and carefully transfer the squash to a cutting board. Remove and discard the bay leaves and cheese rind. On your pressure cooker, select Sauté or Browning, stir in the remaining tomato paste and simmer until the sauce thickens. Season with salt and pepper.

8. Halve the spaghetti squash widthwise and remove the seeds and guts. Use a fork to scrape out the strands. Serve the "spaghetti" topped with the meat sauce.

Penne alla Vodka

My first experience with "pink sauce" was many years ago on Long Island, New York. I was visiting with a friend and his family for a 50th birthday party. Frank Sinatra was playing in the background, so all was right with the world.

PREP: 10 MIN.
COOK: 3 MIN.
YIELD: 4 SERVINGS

46 ounces (794 g) San Marzano whole tomatoes
2 tablespoons (28 g) salted butter
1 teaspoon extra-virgin olive oil
½ cup (40 g) pancetta, diced
2 large shallots, diced
2 garlic cloves, minced
½ cup (120 ml) vodka, divided
16 ounces (454 g) penne pasta (see TOG Tip!)
3 cups (720 ml) water
1 teaspoon salt
Pinch red pepper flakes
¾ cup (180 ml) heavy cream
¾ cup (60 g) Asiago or Parmigiano Reggiano cheese, freshly shredded, divided
Freshly ground black pepper, for garnishing
Fresh basil leaves, for garnishing

♥ **TOG TIP!**

If you want to use a different type of pasta, use the shorter cooking time stated on the package and subtract 3 minutes.

1. Add the tomatoes and their liquid to a food processor and pulse until chunky.

2. On your pressure cooker, select Sauté or Browning and fully heat the cooking pot.

3. Add the butter, olive oil, pancetta, shallots, and garlic to the cooking pot. Sauté for 3 minutes.

4. Pour in ¼ cup (60 ml) of the vodka and deglaze the cooking pot, scraping up any browned bits from the bottom of the pot.

5. Add the tomatoes, pasta, water, salt, and red pepper flakes.

6. Lock the lid and close the pressure valve. Cook for 3 minutes on High Pressure. When the beep sounds, wait 5 minutes, then carefully toggle the pressure valve back and forth to slowly release the remaining pressure.

7. Remove the lid and stir in the remaining ¼ cup (60 ml) vodka. At this point, the pasta will be undercooked in order to simmer the vodka without worry of overcooking the pasta. Select Sauté or Browning and simmer for 2 minutes for perfectly al dente pasta. If you prefer a softer noodle, simmer longer.

8. Stir in the cream and ½ cup (50 g) of cheese, and simmer until the pasta reaches desired tenderness.

9. Garnish with the remaining ¼ cup (25 g) cheese, the black pepper, and basil.

GRAINS AND LEGUMES

PERFECTLY COOKED POT-IN-POT RICE

WHITE RICE *Brown Rice*

THAI TRIPLE COCONUT RICE

PISTACHIO COUSCOUS PILAF

Orange Couscous Pilaf

FRIJOLES NEGROS

VEGETARIAN FRIJOLES

White Rice

Incredibly easy and perfect every time, this recipe will have you falling in love with your pressure cooker over and over again! Use water, broth, tomato juice, and/or any type of liquid and seasonings, and customize your rice to pair with your entrée.

PREP: 5 MIN.
COOK: 3 MIN.
YIELD: 6 SERVINGS

16 ounces (454 g) rice (jasmine, white, Calrose, or basmati), rinsed until the water runs clear
2 cups (475 ml) water (see TOG Tips!)
2 teaspoons sea salt

🤍 **TOG TIPS!**

Substitute the water with broth (chicken, vegetable, beef, etc.), if desired.

The 10 minutes of "natural pressure release" is what steams the rice to perfection.

1. In the pressure cooker cooking pot, combine the rinsed rice and water.

2. Lock the lid and close the pressure valve. Cook for 3 minutes on High Pressure. When the beep sounds, wait 10 minutes, then release the remaining pressure (see TOG Tips!)

3. Remove the lid and season with sea salt.

Brown Rice

Never has brown rice cooked so fast. Nutty, chewy, and full of fiber, brown rice makes a great side to any dish.

PREP: 5 MIN.
COOK: 17 MIN.
YIELD: 6 SERVINGS

14 ounces (400 g) brown rice, rinsed until the water runs clear
2 cups (475 ml) water (see TOG Tip!)

🤍 **TOG TIP!**

For a softer texture, add an additional ¼ cup (60 ml) water.

1. In the pressure cooker cooking pot, combine the rice and water.

2. Lock the lid and close the pressure valve. Cook for 17 minutes on High Pressure. When the beep sounds, wait 10 minutes, then release the remaining pressure.

Perfectly Cooked Pot-in-Pot Rice

PREP: 5 MIN.
COOK: 6 MIN.
YIELD: 4 SERVINGS

This recipe can be used to easily turn many dishes into a pot-in-pot meal (page 9).

1½ cups (360 ml) water
12 ounces (340 g) rice, such as jasmine, white, or basmati, rinsed until the water runs clear
1½ cups (360 ml) chicken broth

♥ TOG TIPS!

This recipe can be used to make any recipe a pot-in-pot meal if the pressure cooking time is between 3 and 10 minutes total.

Do not add any additional water to the cooking pot. NOTE: The 1½ cups (360 ml) of water is only needed when cooking this recipe as a stand-alone recipe.

1. Place a long-legged stainless-steel trivet into the pressure cooker cooking pot and add the water to the pot.

2. Add the rice and broth to the rice pan to a flat-bottom, stainless steel pan. Place the pan on the trivet.

3. Lock the lid and close the pressure valve. Cook for 6 minutes on High Pressure. When the beep sounds, wait 10 minutes, then release the remaining pressure.

3. Fluff the rice with a fork and serve.

Thai Triple Coconut Rice

PREP: 5 MIN.
COOK: 3 MIN.
YIELD: 6 SERVINGS

This rice is fragrant, rich, moderately sweet, and creamy.

12 ounces (340 g) jasmine rice, rinsed until the water runs clear
1 can (14 ounces, or 425 ml) coconut milk
½ cup (120 ml) water
1 tablespoon (15 ml) coconut cream
2 teaspoons coconut sugar (or demerara sugar, raw sugar, or granulated sugar)
½ teaspoon sea salt
Splash vanilla extract (optional)
Coconut flakes, toasted or untoasted, for garnishing

1. In the pressure cooker cooking pot, combine the rice, coconut milk, water, coconut cream, coconut sugar, sea salt, and the tiniest splash of vanilla (if using).

2. Lock the lid and close the pressure valve. Cook for 3 minutes on High Pressure. When the beep sounds, wait 10 minutes, then release the remaining pressure.

3. Remove the lid, fluff the rice with a fork, and top with coconut flakes.

Pistachio Couscous Pilaf

PREP: 10 MIN.
COOK: 0 MIN.
YIELD: 4 SERVINGS

Nutty and fruity, this couscous pairs well with fish, lamb chops, and Middle Eastern–style dishes.

1 tablespoon (15 ml) extra-virgin olive oil
2 large onions, finely diced
1 large red bell pepper, finely diced
1 large carrot, peeled and diced
2 garlic cloves, minced
1½ cups (360 ml) water or chicken broth
2 cups (350 g) couscous
½ cup (75 g) golden raisins
2 teaspoons kosher salt
⅛ teaspoon allspice
Pinch ground cinnamon
¼ cup (16 g) fresh mint leaves, chopped
½ cup pistachios (62 g), pine nuts (68 g),
   or hazelnuts (68 g), chopped

1. On your pressure cooker, select Sauté or Browning and fully heat the cooking pot.

2. Add the olive oil, onions, red bell pepper, and carrot to the cooking pot. Sauté for 5 minutes, or until the onions are soft.

3. Add the garlic and sauté for 1 minute more.

4. Pour in the water and deglaze the cooking pot, scraping up any browned bits from the bottom of the pot.

5. Stir in the couscous, raisins, kosher salt, allspice, and cinnamon.

6. Lock the lid and close the pressure valve. Cook for 0 minutes on High Pressure. When the beep sounds, wait 15 minutes, then release the remaining pressure.

7. Remove the lid and fluff the couscous with a fork. Stir in the mint and pistachios.

Orange Couscous Pilaf

PREP: 5 MIN.
COOK: 0 MIN.
YIELD: 4 SERVINGS

Couscous is very popular in Jewish cooking and can be seasoned similarly to rice pilaf. Have fun and change up the ingredients to suit your taste buds.

2 cups (350 g) couscous

1½ cups (360 ml) freshly squeezed orange juice

½ cup (120 ml) water

1 tablespoon (14 g) salted butter

½ teaspoon kosher salt

2 ounces (55 g) dried currants

1 ounce (28 g) almonds, sliced

1. In your pressure cooker cooking pot, combine the couscous, orange juice, water, butter, kosher salt, and currants.

2. Lock the lid and close the pressure valve. Cook for 0 minutes on High Pressure. When the beep sounds, wait 15 minutes, then release the remaining pressure.

3. Remove the lid and fluff the couscous with a fork.

4. Stir in the almonds right before serving.

Frijoles Negros
(Cuban-Style Black Beans)

PREP: 15 MIN.
COOK: 20 MIN.
YIELD: 6 SERVINGS

Black beans served with rice is a staple in every Cuban household. Growing up in Miami, I ate a lot of black beans at home and in restaurants.
Sofrito is frequently used as a base in Latin American, Spanish, Italian, and Portuguese cooking; Cuban sofrito consists of Spanish onions, green peppers, and garlic.

1 teaspoon extra-virgin olive oil
1 large smoked ham hock (see TOG Tips!)
12 ounces (340 g) Spanish onion, chopped
12 ounces (340 g) green bell pepper, chopped
4 garlic cloves, minced
2 tablespoons (32 g) tomato paste
2½ teaspoons ground cumin
1 teaspoon sugar
1 pound (454 g) dried black beans, rinsed, drained, and picked over (see TOG Tips!)
1 bay leaf
2 quarts (1.9 L) water
Sea salt, to taste (optional)
Cooked rice, for serving

💙 **TOG TIPS!**

For a different flavor profile, use 8 ounces (225 g) chopped bacon instead of the ham hock and add 2 tablespoons (30 g) packed light brown sugar.

Older beans won't cook as fast, or not at all. If the beans are hard after releasing the pressure, lock the lid and cook for an additional 10 minutes. If the beans are still hard, they are probably just too old.

1. On your pressure cooker, select Sauté or Browning and fully heat the cooking pot.

2. Add the olive oil to coat the bottom of the cooking pot.

3. Add the ham hock, onion, and green bell pepper. Sauté for 5 minutes.

4. Add the garlic, tomato paste, cumin, and sugar. Sauté for 30 seconds more.

5. Stir in the black beans, bay leaf, and water.

6. Lock the lid and close the pressure valve. Cook for 20 minutes on High Pressure. When the beep sounds, allow a natural pressure release.

7. Remove the lid and transfer about 1 cup (100 g) black beans to a small bowl. Mash them well with a fork and stir the mashed beans back into the pot. Mashing some of the beans gives the dish a perfect consistency. Taste and season with salt, if needed.

8. Select Sauté or Browning and simmer the beans for 5 minutes more. Remove the bay leaf. Serve with rice.

Vegetarian Frijoles
(Refried Beans)

PREP: 15 MIN.
COOK: 45 MIN.
YIELD: 4 SERVINGS

Pressure-cooker refried beans are a delicious, quick, and healthy side dish or main course. These are wonderful over rice and in burritos and salads.

1 tablespoon (15 ml) extra-virgin olive oil
¼ cup (40 g) onion, diced
3 garlic cloves, minced
¼ teaspoon coriander seeds
2 serrano chiles, stemmed, seeded, and diced
16 ounces (454 g) dried pinto beans, rinsed, drained, and picked over
2 teaspoons sea salt
½ teaspoon ground cumin
⅛ teaspoon chipotle chile seasoning
1 teaspoon True Lime Crystallized (Lime, Garlic & Cilantro; see TOG Tip!)
1 teaspoon distilled white vinegar
3 cups (700 ml) water

1. On your pressure cooker, select Sauté or Browning and fully heat the cooking pot.

2. Add the olive oil to the cooking pot.

3. Add the onion, garlic, coriander seeds, and serrano chiles. Sauté for 2 minutes.

4. Add the beans, sea salt, cumin, chipotle chile, True Lime, vinegar, and water.

5. Lock the lid and close the pressure valve. Cook for 45 minutes on High Pressure. When the beep sounds, wait 10 minutes, then release the remaining pressure.

6. Remove the lid, and using an immersion blender, process the beans to the desired texture.

7. If there is too much liquid, select Sauté or Browning and cook, stirring, until desired consistency is reached.

💙 **TOG TIP!**
True Lime Crystallized is a citrus-based seasoning that adds a huge flavor boost.

APPETIZERS AND SIDES

CAULIFLOWER SOUFFLÉ BAKED BEANS

SUMMER PICNIC POTATO SALAD

Buttermilk Corn Bread Cake

BUFFY'S CARROT MASH

SWEET POTATO CASSEROLE

CREAMY GOAT CHEESE POLENTA

YUCA CON

MOJO *Corn on the Cob*

SOUTHERN-STYLE COLLARD GREENS

SIMPLE SWEET ACORN SQUASH

SOUTHERN-STYLE BOILED PEANUTS *Applesauce*

AND STEAMED BEETS

Cauliflower Soufflé

A delicious, rich, low-carb, keto, and gluten-free side dish, this soufflé makes a great substitute for mashed potatoes—healthy eating without giving up taste. It pairs well with beef, pork, and lamb.

PREP: 10 MIN.
COOK: 15 MIN.
YIELD: 6 SERVINGS

2 tablespoons (28 g) plus 1 teaspoon salted butter, divided

1 head cauliflower, leaves and core removed and cut into large chunks

1 cup (115 g) sharp Cheddar cheese, shredded, plus more for garnishing

½ cup (40 g) Asiago cheese, shredded

½ cup (115 g) sour cream or Yogurt (page 24)

2 ounces (55 g) cream cheese, at room temperature

2 large eggs

2 tablespoons (30 ml) heavy cream

1 teaspoon kosher salt

¼ teaspoon freshly ground black pepper

¼ cup (12 g) fresh chives, chopped, plus more for garnishing

1 cup (240 ml) water

6 bacon slices, cooked and crumbled

1. Grease a 1½-quart (1.4 L) casserole dish with 1 teaspoon of the butter. Set aside.

2. In a food processor, combine the remaining 2 tablespoons (28 g) of butter with the cauliflower, Cheddar and Asiago cheeses, sour cream, cream cheese, eggs, heavy cream, kosher salt, and pepper. Process until smooth.

3. Remove the blade and fold in the chives. Transfer the mixture to the prepared dish.

4. Place a stainless-steel trivet into the pressure cooker cooking pot and add the water to the pot. Place the casserole dish on the trivet.

5. Lock the lid and close the pressure valve. Cook for 15 minutes on High Pressure. When the beep sounds, wait 10 minutes, then release the remaining pressure.

6. Garnish with chives, Cheddar cheese, and crumbled bacon.

Baked Beans

A sweet, sticky sauce makes these baked beans shine at any summer picnic.

1 pound (454 g) dried navy beans
6 to 8 slices thick-cut bacon, roughly chopped
3¼ cups (760 ml) water, divided
1 medium onion, roughly chopped
¼ cup (80 g) real maple syrup
⅓ cup (112 g) molasses
¼ cup (50 g) packed dark brown sugar
⅓ cup (80 g) ketchup
1 tablespoon (15 ml) Worcestershire sauce
1¼ teaspoons dry mustard
¼ teaspoon freshly ground black pepper
1 teaspoon sea salt

1. Rinse and sort the beans, removing any debris. Place the beans in a large bowl and cover with water, 2 inches (5 cm) above the beans. Soak the beans for 3 hours, then drain and rinse (see TOG Tips!).

2. On your pressure cooker, select Sauté or Browning and fully heat the cooking pot.

3. Add the bacon to the cooking pot and cook until the bacon begins to render, scraping up any browned bits from the bottom of the pot. Add ¼ cup (60 ml) of the water and continue cooking until the water has evaporated and the bacon fat is rendered.

4. Add the beans, onion, remaining 3 cups (700 ml) water, maple syrup, molasses, brown sugar, ketchup, Worcestershire sauce, dry mustard, and black pepper, and stir to combine.

5. Lock the lid and close the pressure valve. Cook for 55 minutes on High Pressure.

6. When the beep sounds, wait 15 minutes, then releases the remaining pressure.

7. Add the sea salt. If the beans are still hard, pressure-cook for another 15 minutes. To thicken the liquid, select Sauté or Browning and simmer until desired thickness.

💗 TOG TIPS!

If you have no time to soak the beans, add 15 minutes to the cook time.

If your beans are not very fresh, you may have to cook them longer.

The liquid will continue to thicken as the beans sit.

Summer Picnic Potato Salad

Pressure-cooker potato salad is quick and easy to make. The deviled egg–style dressing makes this the best potato salad around.

PREP: 30 MIN.
COOK: 4 MIN.
YIELD: 6 SERVINGS

2½ pounds (1.1 kg) russet potatoes, peeled and cut into 2-inch (5 cm) cubes
1½ cups (360 ml) water, plus more for the potatoes
Salted butter, for greasing the pan
4 to 6 large eggs
¾ cup (175 g) mayonnaise
1 celery rib, chopped
¼ cup (25 g) scallion, chopped
2 tablespoons (8 g) fresh flat-leaf parsley leaves, chopped
2 tablespoons (18 g) chopped dill pickle
1 tablespoon (11 g) yellow mustard
1 tablespoon (4 g) chopped fresh dill weed (optional)
2 teaspoons TOG House Seasoning (page 10), or to taste
1 teaspoon dill pickle juice
½ teaspoon sea salt
½ to 1 teaspoon paprika

💙 **TOG TIPS!**

Soaking the potatoes in water prior to cooking will remove the starch and produce a better tasting potato.

If not using a loaf pan, place the whole eggs on top of the potatoes in the cooking pot. After cooking, peel and slice or chop the eggs, and combine with the potatoes and dressing.

1. In a large bowl, combine the cubed potatoes with enough water to cover. Soak for 30 minutes (see TOG Tips!).

2. Generously grease a loaf pan with butter. Crack the eggs into the loaf pan (see TOG Tips!).

3. Add the 1½ cups (360 ml) water to the pressure cooker cooking pot.

4. Drain the potatoes and place them in a steamer basket. Put the steamer basket into the cooking pot and place the loaf pan on top of the basket.

5. Lock the lid and close the pressure valve. Cook for 4 minutes on High Pressure. When the beep sounds, carefully toggle the pressure valve and release the remaining pressure.

6. While the potatoes and eggs cook, in a medium bowl, combine the mayonnaise, celery, scallion, parsley, pickle, mustard, dill (if using), house seasoning, pickle juice, and sea salt. Set aside.

7. Remove the lid and transfer the potatoes to a large bowl. Remove the eggs from the loaf pan and place on a baking rack.

8. Add the dressing to the potatoes and carefully incorporate.

9. Place the baking rack over the bowl of potatoes and push the egg through the grates or chop the eggs and add them to the bowl. Gently stir to combine. Sprinkle the potato salad with paprika.

10. Cover the bowl with plastic wrap and refrigerate for at least 2 hours before serving.

Buttermilk Corn Bread Cake

PREP: 20 MIN.
COOK: 20 MIN.
YIELD: 8 SERVINGS

A fluffy change from the traditional Southern-style cast-iron skillet corn bread (which should ONLY be cooked in cast iron and in the oven), this recipe has a cake texture.

Corn Bread

1 cup (125 g) all-purpose flour
(for best results, weigh the flour)
1 cup (140 g) yellow cornmeal
3 tablespoons (36 g) sugar
2½ teaspoons baking powder
½ teaspoon salt
2 large eggs
1 cup (240 ml) buttermilk (see TOG Tips!)
¼ cup (55 g) salted butter, at room temperature, plus more for greasing the pan
1 cup (240 ml) water

Honey Butter

½ cup (120 g, or 1 stick) butter, at room temperature
¼ cup (85 g) honey
½ teaspoon vanilla extract

💛 TOG TIPS!

If you don't have buttermilk, add 1 teaspoon vinegar to a glass measuring cup and pour in enough milk to reach the 1-cup (240 ml) line. Stir and let sit for 5 minutes.

Letting the batter sit for 15 minutes, helps to give the corn bread a better head.

For a spicy version, add chopped jalapeños or other chile peppers, and a sprinkle of Cajun seasoning; for a cheesy version, mix in ½ cup (58 g) shredded Cheddar cheese and chopped green chiles (optional).

1. **To make the corn bread:** In a large bowl, combine the flour, cornmeal, sugar, baking powder, and salt.

2. In a medium bowl, whisk together the eggs, buttermilk, and butter.

3. Pour the flour mixture into the egg mixture and gently stir until just combined. Do not overwork the batter. Let sit for 15 minutes (see TOG Tips!).

4. Grease a 6-inch (15 cm) PushPan or springform pan with butter and pour in the batter. Cover the pan with a lid or aluminum foil.

5. Place a stainless steel trivet into the pressure cooker cooking pot and add the water to the pot. Using a foil sling, lower the pan onto the trivet.

6. Lock the lid and close the pressure valve. Cook for 20 minutes on High Pressure. When the beep sounds, wait 10 minutes, then release the remaining pressure.

7. **To make the honey butter:** Add the butter, honey, and vanilla to a medium bowl. Use a whisk to whip the butter. Refrigerate once prepared.

8. Serve the corn bread with the honey butter.

Buffy's Carrot Mash

PREP: 10 MIN.
COOK: 7 MIN.
YIELD: 4–6 SERVINGS

In 1985, shortly after moving to California, I met some friends while walking my cocker spaniel, Buffy; they were walking Puggy, their pug. The first time I had dinner with them, this side dish was served. It's healthier alternative to mashed potatoes, and the carrots add beautiful color and a hint of sweetness.

1 cup (240 ml) water, for the cooking pot
3 large russet potatoes, unpeeled,
   cut into 2-inch (5 cm) cubes
8 large carrots, peeled and cut into
   1½-inch (4 cm) cubes (see TOG Tip!)
½ cup (120 ml) milk, plus more as needed
2 teaspoons sea salt, or to taste
2 tablespoons (28 g) salted butter,
   or to taste

💗 **TOG TIP!**
The carrots should be cut into smaller pieces than the potatoes.

1. Place a stainless-steel trivet into the pressure cooker cooking pot and add the water to the pot. Place the potatoes and carrots in a strainer basket and place in the cooking pot.

2. Lock the lid and close the pressure valve. Cook for 7 minutes on High Pressure. When the beep sounds, wait 5 minutes, then release the remaining pressure.

3. Remove the lid and transfer the potatoes and carrots to a large bowl. Mash with a fork.

4. Add the milk and continue to mash. If you want a creamier texture, add a little more milk.

5. Add the sea salt and mash until completely combined.

6. Stir in the butter and combine well. Dot with additional butter, if desired.

Creamy Goat Cheese Polenta

PREP: 5 MIN.
COOK: 5 MIN.
YIELD: 6 SERVINGS

"Dreamy" is the best way to describe this recipe. It is rich and smooth, and a great alternative to mashed potatoes. It pairs well with red meat, such as the Red Wine–Braised Short Ribs (page 74) or a stew.

4 cups (960 ml) water
1 cup (140 g) cornmeal
2 tablespoons (28 g) salted butter
1 teaspoon sea salt
Pinch cayenne pepper
3 ounces (85 g) goat cheese
   (see TOG Tips!)

1. To your pressure cooker cooking pot, add the water, cornmeal, butter, sea salt, and cayenne pepper.

2. Lock the lid and close the pressure valve. Cook for 5 minutes on High Pressure. When the beep sounds, wait 10 minutes, then release the remaining pressure.

3. Remove the lid and select Sauté or Browning. Simmer until desired thickness is reached.

4. Add the goat cheese and stir until melted.

♡ TOG TIPS!

Feta, cotija, or any other crumbly cheese can be used instead of goat cheese.

For polenta patties, cook down the polenta until it is very thick and place it in the refrigerator. When chilled, form it into hockey puck–size disks and fry in oil or butter in a cast-iron skillet for 2 minutes, or until browned and crisp.

Corn on the Cob: Two Methods

PREP: 5 MIN.
COOK: 1 MIN.
YIELD: 4 SERVINGS

Corn on the cob can be traditionally cooked on a steamer rack or in the pot for a butter-infused flavor.

Steam Method

1 cup (240 ml) water
4 ears corn (or more), fresh or frozen, husks and silk removed, if fresh (see TOG Tip!)

"Flavor-Bomb" Method

4 ears corn (or more), fresh or frozen, husks and silk removed, if fresh (see Good Old Tip!)
1 cup (240 ml) water
½ cup (120 ml) milk
1 tablespoon (13 g) sugar
2 tablespoons (28 g) salted butter
1 teaspoon sea salt

🤍 TOG TIP!

If you want to cook the corn with the husks on, add 2 minutes to the cooking time.

For the steam method:

1. Place a stainless-steel trivet into the pressure cooker cooking pot and add the water to the pot. Place the corn on the trivet.

2. Lock the lid and close the pressure valve. Cook for 1 minute on High Pressure. If using frozen corn, cook for 0 to 1 minute. When the beep sounds, wait 5 minutes, then release the remaining pressure.

For the "flavor-bomb" method:

1. To the pressure cooker cooking pot, add the corn, water, milk, sugar, butter, and sea salt.

2. Lock the lid and close the pressure valve. Cook for 1 minute on High Pressure. If using frozen corn, cook for 0 to 1 minute. Wait 15 minutes for all the pressure to be released. The longer the corn sits in the liquid, the more it becomes infused with flavor.

Yuca con Mojo

PREP: 10 MIN.
COOK: 12 MIN.
YIELD: 4–6 SERVINGS

Yuca (cassava) and *malanga* are two of my favorite side dishes to eat with Cuban food. With my method, this yuca con mojo is super simple. The yuca is cooked at the same time as the sour orange garlic sauce, all in one pot.

2 pounds (907 g) yuca or malanga
   (see TOG Tips!)
2 tablespoons (30 ml) extra-virgin olive oil
¼ cup (60 g) onion, thickly sliced
6 garlic cloves, roughly chopped
1 tablespoon (14 g) salted butter
1 teaspoon sea salt
½ cup (120 ml) freshly squeezed orange
   juice (see TOG Tips!)
½ cup (120 ml) freshly squeezed lime
   juice (see TOG Tips!)
Fresh parsley leaves or cilantro leaves,
   for garnishing (optional)

🤍 TOG TIPS!

Frozen yuca (or malanga) can be used. It is usually peeled and frozen raw.

If you don't have fresh citrus, True Lime and True Orange, citrus-based seasonings, work equally as well. Mix 4 teaspoons into 1 cup (240 ml) water for each flavor.

1. With a sharp knife, trim the ends of the yuca and cut it into 2 or 3 pieces. Stand the yuca on end and cut off the peel. Quarter the pieces lengthwise and cut out the woody core. Place the yuca in a steamer basket.

2. On your pressure cooker, select Sauté or Browning and fully heat the cooking pot.

3. Add the olive oil and onion to the cooking pot, and sauté for 3 minutes. Add the garlic and butter, and sauté for 30 seconds.

4. Stir in the sea salt, orange juice, and lime juice.

5. Place the steamer basket with the yuca into the cooking pot. Lock the lid and close the pressure valve. Cook for 12 minutes on High Pressure. When the beep sounds, wait 10 minutes, then release the remaining pressure.

6. Remove the lid and transfer the yuca from the steamer basket into the sauce in the cooking pot. Select Sauté or Browning and simmer to thicken the sauce.

7. Place the yuca and sauce in a bowl and garnish with parsley (if using).

Traditional Sweet Potato Casserole

PREP: 15 MIN.
COOK: 17 MIN.
YIELD: 8 SERVINGS

This traditional casserole has yams or sweet potatoes with a surprise and is ideal for the winter holidays.

Filling
¼ cup (29 g) Grape-Nuts cereal
¼ cup (25 g) packed light brown sugar

Casserole
½ cup (112 g) salted butter, plus more for greasing the casserole dish
2 cups (480 ml) water, divided, for the cooking pot
2 pounds (907 g) sweet potatoes or yams, peeled and chopped
1 large egg
½ teaspoon ground cinnamon
½ teaspoon sea salt
Pinch ground nutmeg
8 ounces (225 g) marshmallows
¼ to ½ cup (25 to 50 g) packed light brown sugar

💜 **TOG TIPS!**

Use a 7-inch (18 cm) casserole dish for 6-quart (5.6 L) or larger pressure cookers; use a 7- to 9-inch (18 to 23 cm) casserole dish for 8-quart (7.5 L) or larger pressure cookers; and double the recipe for an 8- or 9-inch (20 or 23 cm) casserole dish.

For single servings (like in the photo), cook for 7 minutes.

1. **To make the filling:** In a small bowl, combine the Grape-Nuts and brown sugar. Set aside.

2. **To make the casserole:** Grease a 1½-quart (1.4 L) casserole dish with butter and set aside (see TOG Tips!).

3. Add 1 cup (240 ml) of the water to the pressure cooker cooking pot. Add the sweet potatoes to a steamer basket and place it in the cooking pot.

4. Lock the lid and close the pressure valve. Cook for 4 minutes on High Pressure. When the beep sounds, wait 5 minutes, then release the remaining pressure. Keep the water in the pot.

5. Transfer the sweet potatoes to a large bowl. Add the ½ cup (112 g) butter, egg, cinnamon, sea salt, and nutmeg. With a handheld electric mixer, whip everything to combine.

6. Pour half of the sweet potato mixture into the prepared casserole dish. Sprinkle the filling evenly over the top. Gently spoon the remaining sweet potato mixture over the filling.

7. Place the stainless steel trivet into the pressure cooker and add the remaining 1 cup (240 ml) water to your cooking pot. Using a foil sling, lower the dish into the cooking pot.

8. Lock the lid and close the pressure valve. Cook for 13 minutes on High Pressure (see TOG Tips!). When the beep sounds, do a quick pressure release. Remove the lid and the casserole dish.

9. Top the sweet potatoes with the marshmallows. Place the casserole under the broiler (or in an air fryer) for 1 to 2 minutes, or until desired color is achieved.

Southern-Style Collard Greens

PREP: 15 MIN.
COOK: 40 MIN.
YIELD: 4 SERVINGS

During my years living in Charleston, South Carolina, I picked up some recipes and tips for Southern cooking. Collard greens cooked in ham broth is a Southern staple and quite easy to prepare.

1 ham hock
1½ cups (360 ml) chicken stock or water
1 pound (454 g) fresh collard greens, washed well and trimmed
1 medium onion, chopped
2 garlic cloves, minced
2 tablespoons (30 ml) apple cider vinegar
1 tablespoon packed light brown sugar (15 g) or honey (20 g)
2 teaspoons kosher salt
1 teaspoon freshly ground black pepper
1 teaspoon Sambal Oelek Ground Fresh Chili Paste or hot pepper sauce
1 teaspoon smoked paprika

1. Place the ham hock and chicken stock into the pressure cooker cooking pot.

2. Lock the lid and close the pressure valve. Cook for 15 minutes on High Pressure (see TOG Tip!). When the beep sounds, wait 5 minutes, then release the remaining pressure.

3. Remove the lid and add the collard greens, onion, garlic, vinegar, brown sugar, kosher salt, black pepper, chili paste, and smoked paprika to the cooking pot.

4. Lock the lid and close the pressure valve. Cook for 25 minutes on High Pressure. When the beep sounds, allow a natural pressure release.

5. Remove the lid and transfer the ham hock to a cutting board. Separate the meat and skin/fat from the bone.

6. Return just the meat to the cooking pot and combine with the greens. Simmer, if desired, to cook down the liquid.

🩶 TOG TIP!

This longer cook time for the ham hock yields a very flavorful broth. If you are in a rush, just combine all the ingredients in the cooking pot and cook for 25 minutes.

Simple Sweet Acorn Squash

PREP: 5 MIN.
COOK: 4 MIN.
YIELD: 2 SERVINGS

This recipe can be used for other varieties of squash, such as butternut, delicata, and pumpkin.

1 tablespoon (14 g) salted butter, at room temperature

1 tablespoon (15 g) packed light brown sugar

¼ teaspoon ground cinnamon

Pinch kosher salt, or to taste

Pinch freshly ground black pepper, or to taste

1 acorn squash, halved and seeds and pulp removed

1 cup (240 ml) water, for the cooking pot

Freshly grated nutmeg, for dusting (optional)

1. In a small bowl, combine the butter, brown sugar, cinnamon, kosher salt, and black pepper. Top each squash half with one-half of the seasonings.

2. Place a stainless-steel trivet into the pressure cooker cooking pot and add the water to the pot. Carefully place the squash halves on the trivet.

3. Lock the lid and close the pressure valve. Cook for 4 minutes on High Pressure; for a softer texture, cook for 5 to 7 minutes. When the beep sounds, wait 10 minutes, then release the remaining pressure.

4. Serve dusted with nutmeg, if desired.

Southern-Style Boiled Peanuts

PREP: 5 MIN.
COOK: 65 MIN.
YIELD: 4 SERVINGS

Boiled peanuts make a wonderful snack. From the first time I cracked open a boiled peanut and tasted the salty brine and the soft nut, I was hooked. I like to leave the peanuts in the cooking water and take them out with a strainer. Serve in a brown-paper lunch bag like at the roadside stands.

1 pound (454 g) jumbo raw peanuts in the shell
½ cup (118 g) sea salt
Water, to cover the peanuts

1. Rinse the peanuts under cool water and remove any twigs, roots, or whatever does not belong.

2. In your pressure cooker cooking pot, combine the peanuts, salt, and enough water to cover. Place a plate or stainless-steel trivet on top of the peanuts to keep them submerged.

3. Lock the lid and close the pressure valve. Cook for 65 minutes on High Pressure. When the beep sounds, allow a natural pressure release and let sit 30 minutes or longer.

4. Remove the lid and test for doneness. If the peanuts are too hard for your liking, relock the lid, close the pressure valve, and cook longer (see TOG Tips!).

💙 **TOG TIPS!**

You may need to cook the peanuts longer, depending on your preference. My sweet spot is 65 minutes; others prefer up to 2 hours.

For a Cajun twist, add 1 tablespoon (15 ml) Cajun seasoning, 4 garlic cloves, and 2 jalapeño peppers; for a barbecue burst, add 1 tablespoon (15 ml) barbecue seasoning and 1 teaspoon sugar.

For Asian-style peanuts, like those found on the streets of China, use ¼ cup (60 g) sea salt and add 3 star anise, 3 cinnamon sticks, 3 garlic cloves, 1 chunk rock sugar, and 4 dried red chile peppers to the cooking liquid.

Applesauce

Homemade applesauce is so simple to make. Choose the apple types you enjoy most. Sometimes I also add whatever fruit is in season; pears, raspberries, strawberries, mango, and cherries are all wonderful additions.

PREP: 15 MIN.
COOK: 3 MIN.
YIELD: 8 SERVINGS

10 large apples (a combination such as Honeycrisp, Red Delicious, Braeburn, Pink Lady, Granny Smith), cored, quartered, and peeled or unpeeled (see TOG Tip!)

1-inch (2.5 cm) piece fresh ginger, peeled and grated, or $1/8$ teaspoon ground ginger

$1/8$ teaspoon ground cinnamon

Pinch nutmeg

Juice of 1 lemon

2 to 4 tablespoons honey (40 to 80 g) or packed light brown sugar (30 to 60 g), if needed

1. In your pressure cooker cooking pot, combine the apples with the ginger, cinnamon, nutmeg, and lemon juice.

2. Lock the lid and close the pressure valve. Cook for 3 minutes on High Pressure. When the beep sounds, allow a full natural pressure release.

3. Remove the lid and use an immersion blender to process the apples to your desired texture.

4. Taste and add honey for sweetness if needed. Transfer to an airtight container and refrigerate for up to 1 week.

🤍 **TOG TIP!**

Granny Smith apples are very tart; if you use them, you may need to add ¼ cup honey (80 g) or brown sugar (60 g). If adding other fruit to the cooking pot, taste after blending, before adding a sweetener.

Steamed Beets

Sliced fresh beets add a warm and earthy taste to garden salads.
I especially love blue cheese on a salad with beets.

PREP: 10 MIN.
COOK: 9 MIN.
YIELD: 4–6 SERVINGS

6 to 10 medium beets, washed and
scrubbed, and root ends trimmed;
do not peel (see TOG Tip!)

1½ cups (360 ml) water, for the
cooking pot

1. Place the beets in a steamer basket. Add the water to the pressure cooker cooking pot and place the steamer basket into the cooking pot.

2. Lock the lid and close the pressure valve. Cook for 9 minutes on High Pressure. When the beep sounds, wait 10 minutes, then release the remaining pressure.

3. Remove the lid and the steamer basket. Place it under cold running water.

4. Rub off the beet skins and slice them or cut them into chunks or wedges.

💚 **TOG TIP!**

*For small beets, cook for 5 minutes;
large beets, 12 minutes; and extra-large
beets, 14 minutes.*

DESSERTS

PEPPERMINT MILKSHAKE CHEESECAKE

New York Cheesecake

MOCHA LATTE MOUSSE

RUM RAISIN RICE PUDDING

EGG CUSTARD *Cherry Clafoutis*

EASY LEMON CURD AND

ITALIAN APPLE OLIVE OIL CAKE

Peppermint Milkshake Cheesecake

PREP: 30 MIN.
COOK: 45 MIN.
YIELD: 8 SERVINGS

Imagine an ice-cream shake on top of a chocolate-cake base. Add in cream cheese and you've got a rich and delicious cheesecake, perfect for a special occasion. The white chocolate mousse adds an extra layer of deliciousness.

Crust

1 tablespoon (14 g) butter, melted, plus more for greasing the pan
25 chocolate wafer cookies (Nabisco Famous, or another crispy cookie)
6 to 10 peppermint candies
1 drop peppermint extract

Filling

16 ounces (454 g) cream cheese, at room temperature
4 ounces (115 g) peppermint bark, chopped
2 candy canes or peppermint candies
¼ cup (50 g) sugar
¼ cup (60 ml) heavy whipping cream
2 tablespoons (30 ml) all-purpose flour
½ teaspoon vanilla extract
½ teaspoon peppermint extract, or to taste
3 large eggs, at room temperature
1½ cups (360 ml) water

Top Layer (see TOG Tips!)

1 large egg yolk
1 tablespoon (15 ml) sugar
4 ounces (115 g) white chocolate melting chips, chopped into small pieces
½ cup (120 ml) plus 2 tablespoons (30 ml) heavy cream
Crushed peppermint candies, for garnishing

1. Place a medium stainless steel bowl in the freezer.

2. **To make the crust:** Generously grease a 6-inch (15 cm) PushPan or springform pan with butter (see TOG Tips!). Place a 6-inch (15 cm) round of parchment paper on the bottom of the pan. Set aside.

3. In a food processor, combine the chocolate wafers and peppermints. Pulse a couple of times until small crumbs form.

4. Add the melted butter and peppermint extract. Pulse until just combined. Pour the crust mixture into the prepared pan and press the mixture firmly onto the bottom of the pan. Freeze the crust for 15 minutes.

5. **To make the filling:** In a blender, combine the cream cheese, peppermint bark, peppermint candies, sugar, heavy cream, flour, and vanilla and peppermint extracts. Blend until smooth.

6. Add the eggs, one at a time, blending until just combined. Do not overmix the eggs. Pour the filling over the crust.

7. Cover the cheesecake first with a paper towel and then with a piece of aluminum foil, and loosely secure the foil.

8. Place a stainless steel trivet into the pressure cooker cooking pot and add the water to the pot. Using a foil sling, lower the cheesecake onto the trivet.

9. Lock the lid and close the pressure valve. Cook for 45 minutes on High Pressure. When the beep sounds, wait 20 minutes, then release the remaining pressure (if any).

(continued on next page)

10. Remove the lid, then gently remove the cheesecake. Remove the foil and paper towel. Slightly tilt the cheesecake and dab off any liquid that may have accumulated with another paper towel. The center should be slightly jiggly, but not liquid. (Heat will be trapped inside the cheesecake and it will continue to cook and firm up; however, if there is uncooked filling on top, put the cheesecake back into the pressure cooker and cook for 5 minutes more on High Pressure. Wait 10 minutes, then release the remaining pressure.)

11. Refrigerate the cheesecake for a full 24 hours to set properly, develop flavor, and become dense.

12. **To make the top layer:** The topping should be made the following day, a couple hours prior to serving. In a small bowl, whisk together the egg yolk and sugar.

13. In a small saucepan over low heat, heat 2 tablespoons (30 ml) of the heavy cream, 1 to 2 minutes. Turn off the heat.

14. Temper the egg yolk: Whisk 1 teaspoon of hot cream into the egg mixture. Add the egg mixture to the warm pan, along with the chopped white chocolate. Whisk until smooth. If the chocolate does not fully melt, turn the heat back on for just a few seconds to warm the ingredients, then turn it back off. Pour the mixture into the chilled bowl.

15. In a medium bowl, whisk the remaining ½ cup (120 ml) cream to form soft peaks. Carefully fold half the whipped cream into the chocolate mixture. Now fold in the remaining whipped cream. Refrigerate for 1 hour to set.

16. Gently spoon the white chocolate mousse over the cheesecake and decorate with crushed candies.

♥ TOG TIPS!

If you don't want to make the white chocolate mousse topping, a sweet cream layer (see New York Cheesecake, page 181) or melted white chocolate chips are also good options.

If you want to use a different size pan, cook times are as follows, all with a full natural pressure release:
- *7-inch (18 cm) pan: 42 minutes*
- *7-inch (18 cm) pan, tall recipe: increase the recipe by half and cook for 50 minutes*
- *8- or 9-inch (20 or 23 cm) pan: double the recipe and cook for 45 minutes*
- *4-inch (10 cm) mini pans: divide the filling among 3 mini pans and cook for 15 minutes*
- *8-ounce (240 ml) wide-mouth glass jar (6 jars): 9 minutes*
- *4-ounce (120 ml) wide-mouth glass jar (12 jars): 6 minutes*
- *16-ounce (475 ml) glass jar: don't do it!*

New York Cheesecake

I'm ashamed to say that I have had a cheesecake obsession most of my life, so it is safe to say that I know cheesecake! Many years ago, my friend brought a cheesecake to work, and after one bite, I knew I was in serious trouble. It was the best I had ever tasted. She gave me her recipe, which I quickly converted for the pressure cooker. Thanks, Phyllis. My fans and my waist also thank you.

PREP: 25 MIN.
COOK: 38 MIN.
YIELD: 8 SERVINGS

Crust

2 tablespoons (28 g) butter, melted, plus more for greasing the pan
¾ cup (15 g) crushed cinnamon or plain graham crackers (see TOG Tips!)
2 teaspoons sugar

Filling

16 ounces (454 g) cream cheese, at room temperature
½ cup (100 g) sugar
¼ cup (60 ml) heavy or whipping cream
2 teaspoons all-purpose flour
1 teaspoon vanilla extract
½ teaspoon orange zest, finely grated, plus more for garnishing (optional)
½ teaspoon lemon zest, finely grated
Pinch sea salt
2 large eggs, at room temperature
1 large egg yolk, at room temperature
1½ cups (360 ml) water

Sweet Cream Topping

½ cup (115 g) sour cream or Yogurt (page 24)
2 teaspoons sugar (you may need more sugar if yogurt is used)
½ teaspoon vanilla extract

1. Generously grease a 6-inch (15 cm) PushPan or springform pan with butter. Place a 6-inch (15 cm) round of parchment paper on the bottom of the pan. Set aside.

2. **To make the crust:** In a food processor, combine the graham cracker crumbs and sugar. Pulse a couple of times until small crumbs form. Add the melted butter. Pulse until just combined. Pour the crust mixture into the prepared pan and press the mixture firmly onto the bottom of the pan. Freeze the crust for 20 minutes.

3. **To make the filling:** In a blender, combine the cream cheese, sugar, heavy cream, flour, orange and lemon peels, vanilla, and sea salt. Blend until smooth.

4. One at a time, add the eggs and egg yolk, blending until just combined. Do not overmix the eggs. Pour the filling over the crust.

5. Cover the cheesecake first with a paper towel and then with a piece of aluminum foil, and loosely secure the foil.

6. Place a stainless steel trivet into the pressure cooker cooking pot and add the water to the pot. Using a foil sling, lower the cheesecake onto the trivet.

7. Lock the lid and close the pressure valve. Cook for 38 minutes on High Pressure. When the beep sounds, wait 18 minutes, then release the remaining pressure (if any). Open the pot and remove the cheesecake.

(continued on next page)

8. Remove the lid, then gently remove the cheesecake. Remove the foil and paper towel. Slightly tilt the cheesecake and dab off any liquid that may have accumulated with another paper towel. The center should be very slightly jiggly, but not liquid. (Heat will be trapped inside the cheesecake and it will continue to cook and firm up; however, if there is uncooked filling on top, put the cheesecake back into the pressure cooker and cook for 5 minutes more on High Pressure. Wait 10 minutes, then release the remaining pressure).

9. **To make the topping:** In a small bowl, whisk together the sour cream, sugar, and vanilla extract. Spread on the hot cheesecake. Cool on a wire rack for 1 hour. Carefully remove only the sides of the pan. Lightly cover the cheesecake with a large pot or bowl and refrigerate for a full 24 hours to set properly, develop flavor, and become dense.

♥ TOG TIPS!

Any kind of crispy cookie crumbs can be used, such as vanilla wafers, shortbread, gingersnaps, chocolate wafers, chocolate sandwich cookies, etc.

If you want to use a different size pan, cook times are as follows, all with a full natural pressure release:
- *7-inch (18 cm) pan: 30 minutes.*
- *7-inch (18 cm) pan, tall recipe: increase the recipe by half and cook for 38 minutes*
- *8- or 9-inch (20 or 23 cm) pan: double the recipe and cook for 40 minutes*
- *4-inch (10 cm) mini pans: divide the filling among 3 mini pans and cook for 12 minutes*
- *5-inch (13 cm) mini pan: 17 minutes*
- *8-ounce (240 ml) wide-mouth glass jar (6 jars): 7 minutes*
- *4-ounce (120 ml) wide-mouth glass jar (12 jars): 4 minutes*
- *16-ounce (475 ml) glass jar: don't do it!*

Mocha Latte Mousse

Light and airy with hints of cinnamon, my mocha latte mousse is an elegant dessert that can be served at the fanciest of dinner parties, and is a great choice for a quick dessert for the family.

PREP: 10 MIN.
COOK: 0 MIN.
YIELD: 8–10 SERVINGS

12 ounces (340 g) milk chocolate chips
1 cup (240 ml) brewed espresso or 1 cup (240 ml) water plus 5 teaspoons instant espresso powder (see TOG Tips!)
1 cinnamon stick
1 teaspoon vanilla extract
4½ cups (1.1 L) heavy whipping cream
Chocolate shavings, for garnishing
Ground cinnamon, for garnishing
Vanilla bean powder, for garnishing

1. To your pressure cooker cooking pot, add the milk chocolate chips, espresso, cinnamon stick, and vanilla.

2. Lock the lid and close the pressure valve. Cook for 0 minutes on Low Pressure. When the beep sounds, turn off the pressure cooker, wait 2 minutes, then release the remaining pressure.

3. Remove the lid and pour the mocha mixture into a medium bowl. Remove and discard the cinnamon stick. Whisk the mixture until completely smooth. Let cool for 15 minutes.

4. In a large bowl, whip the cream until stiff peaks form. Fold the whipped cream into the mocha mixture. Pipe or spoon the mixture among 8 to 10 serving bowls and refrigerate until chilled.

5. Serve garnished with chocolate shavings and a sprinkle of cinnamon and vanilla powders.

♥ **TOG TIPS!**

One cup (240 ml) of strong coffee can be substituted for the espresso, if you prefer a lighter coffee flavor.

For peppermint mocha, add ½ teaspoon peppermint extract and garnish with a peppermint stick.

Rum Raisin Rice Pudding

PREP: 50 MIN.
COOK: 4 MIN.
YIELD: 4 SERVINGS

Imagine if rum raisin ice cream and your favorite rice pudding had a baby. My rum raisin rice pudding is delicious any time of the year and makes a great dessert for any holiday meal.

½ cup (75 g) raisins
½ cup (120 ml) spiced rum
   (see TOG Tips!)
1½ cups (350 ml) water
1 cup (192 g) Arborio rice
1 cinnamon stick
¼ teaspoon sea salt
2½ cups (600 ml) heavy cream, divided
½ cup (100 g) demerara sugar
   (see TOG Tips!)
2 large eggs
½ teaspoon vanilla extract
Whipped cream, for serving (optional)
Ground cinnamon, ground nutmeg,
   pumpkin pie spice, ground cloves,
   for dusting (optional)

1. In a small bowl, combine the raisins and rum. Soak for 45 minutes.

2. In your pressure cooker cooking pot, combine the water, rice, cinnamon stick, and sea salt.

3. Lock the lid and close the pressure valve. Cook for 4 minutes on High Pressure. When the beep sounds, wait 10 minutes, then release the remaining pressure.

4. Remove the lid and add 2 cups (480 ml) of the cream and the sugar, and stir to combine.

5. In a glass measuring cup, combine the eggs, vanilla, and remaining ½ cup (120 ml) cream. Whisk well until frothy. Slowly pour the cream mixture into the cooking pot, stirring as you go.

6. On your pressure cooker, select Sauté or Browning and let the pudding come to a slow boil, stirring constantly. Continue to stir for 1 minute only.

7. Remove the cooking pot from the pressure cooker. Remove the raisins from the rum with a slotted spoon and add to the cooking pot. Add 3 tablespoons (45 ml) of the reserved rum and stir to combine.

8. Enjoy warm or cooled and serve with a dollop of whipped cream, and a sprinkle of cinnamon, nutmeg, pumpkin pie spice, or cloves, if desired.

🤍 TOG TIPS!

While spiced rum is fantastic in this recipe, feel free to use your favorite flavored rum. Grand Marnier, triple sec, and brandy can be used for other flavors of rice pudding.

Coconut, granulated, or raw sugar can be used in place of demerara sugar.

The rice pudding will thicken as it cools.

Egg Custard *(The British Way)*

PREP: 5 MIN.
COOK: 7 MIN.
YIELD: 6 SERVINGS

A classic dessert from the Old World—light, smooth, and airy, this custard can be prepared quickly, especially when you have unexpected company.

6 large eggs
4 cups (960 ml) milk
¾ cup (150 g) sugar
1 teaspoon vanilla extract
Tiniest pinch sea salt
1½ cups (360 ml) water, for the
 cooking pot
Ground cinnamon, for dusting
Freshly grated nutmeg, for dusting
Fresh berries, for topping

1. In a medium bowl, using a handheld electric mixer, beat the eggs. Add the milk, sugar, vanilla, and sea salt, and beat again until combined. Do not overmix. Pour the mixture into a 1.5-quart (1.4 L) flat-bottom, stainless steel pan and cover it with a vented lid or aluminum foil (see TOG Tips!).

2. Place a stainless steel trivet into the pressure cooker cooking pot and add the water to the pot. Place the covered pan on top of the trivet.

3. Lock the lid and close the pressure valve. Cook for 7 minutes on High Pressure. When the beep sounds, wait 10 minutes, then release the remaining pressure.

4. Remove the lid and the custard. Serve topped with a dusting of cinnamon and nutmeg or fresh berries, if desired.

♥ TOG TIPS!

If using a glass bowl, cook for 9 to 10 minutes. For ramekins or custard cups, cover with foil and poke small vent holes in the top. Cook for 2 minutes.

It is essential to use the proper pan insert to achieve a perfect custard in 7 minutes. A longer cooking time for a smaller, but deeper or taller, pan will not work and will make scrambled eggs!

Cherry Clafoutis

PREP: 10 MIN.
COOK: 15 MIN.
YIELD: 6 SERVINGS

This French dessert is ready to serve in less than 30 minutes, so impress your guests with this flan Dutch baby.

2½ teaspoons butter, melted, divided
8 ounces (225 g) fresh dark cherries, pitted (or just enough to cover the bottom of the pan; see TOG Tips!)
¾ cup (90 g) all-purpose flour
3 large eggs
1 egg white
½ cup (120 ml) milk
½ teaspoon distilled white vinegar
6 tablespoons (75 g) sugar, divided
1 tablespoon (15 ml) brandy or kirsch
½ teaspoon almond extract
Pinch sea salt
1½ cups water, for the cooking pot
Confectioners' sugar, for garnishing

♥ TOG TIPS!

Clafoutis is traditionally made with cherries, but berries, peaches, and other fruit can be used. You can also substitute defrosted frozen cherries for the fresh ones.

In a traditional Limousin clafoutis, the pits remain in the cherries during baking. They release a small amount of amygdalin, which is the active chemical in almond extract. It adds a nice flavor, but rather than choke on a pit, I prefer to pit the cherries and add a touch of almond extract.

You can substitute maraschino liqueur or juice for the brandy.

1. Generously grease a 7½-inch round (19 cm) cake pan with ½ teaspoon of the butter.

2. Place the cherries in the pan in a single layer (they should cover the bottom).

3. In a food processor, combine the remaining 2 teaspoons butter, the flour, eggs, egg white, milk, vinegar, 4 tablespoons (50 g) of the sugar, brandy, almond extract, and sea salt. Process until foamy.

4. Pour the mixture over the cherries.

5. Sprinkle with the remaining 2 tablespoons (25 g) sugar and cover with aluminum foil.

6. Place a stainless steel trivet into the pressure cooker cooking pot and add the water to the pot. Using a foil sling, lower the cake pan onto the trivet.

7. Lock the lid and close the pressure valve. Cook for 15 minutes on High Pressure. When the beep sounds, wait 10 minutes, then release the remaining pressure.

8. Remove the lid, then remove the clafoutis from the pressure cooker. The cake will rise and fall, leaving the sides higher than the center. Dust a little confectioners' sugar over the top and serve warm.

Easy Lemon Curd

PREP: 10 MIN.
COOK: 10 MIN.
YIELD: 3 CUPS

Making lemon curd is so simple in the pressure cooker. Sweet and tart, it is delicious on cakes and cupcakes. This recipe can easily be doubled.

6 tablespoons (85 g) unsalted butter
1 cup (200 g) sugar
2 large eggs
2 large egg yolks
2/3 cup (160 ml) freshly squeezed lemon juice
1½ cups (360 ml) water, for the cooking pot
1 to 2 teaspoons grated lemon zest

♥ **TOG TIP!**
Use this recipe and oranges to make orange curd, limes for lime curd, and grapefruit for grapefruit curd.

1. In a food processor or blender, combine the butter and sugar, and process for about 2 minutes, or until completely smooth.

2. Slowly add the eggs and yolks, and process for just 1 minute.

3. Add the lemon juice and process to combine. The mixture will look curdled, but it will smooth out as it cooks. Pour the mixture into a 1-quart (1 L) flat-bottom pan and tightly cover.

4. Place a stainless steel trivet into the pressure cooker cooking pot and add the water to the pot. Using a foil sling, lower the pan onto the trivet.

5. Lock the lid and close the pressure valve. Cook for 10 minutes on High Pressure. When the beep sounds, wait 10 minutes, then release the remaining pressure.

6. Remove the lid, then remove the pan from the pressure cooker. Add the lemon zest and stir the curd until very smooth.

7. Cool for 25 minutes and then refrigerate overnight. The curd will thicken as it cools and will keep, refrigerated, for 1 week or in the freezer for 2 months.

Italian Apple Olive Oil Cake

PREP: 15 MIN.
COOK: 50 MIN.
YIELD: 8 SERVINGS

This is the perfect breakfast cake to eat with your morning coffee or espresso. With its subtle spices and sweet fruit, this traditional cake will be loved by all. For dessert, serve with a scoop of vanilla ice cream, a drizzle of caramel, or a sprinkling of sugar and cinnamon. For an adult cake, soak the raisins in limoncello, rum, or brandy. Walnuts or pecans would add a nice crunch.

1 pound (454 g) Granny Smith apples, peeled and diced

⅔ cup (100 g) golden raisins

1 cup (240 ml) orange juice

2¾ cups (340 g) all-purpose flour (see TOG Tips!)

1½ teaspoons baking powder

1½ teaspoons baking soda

¾ teaspoon ground cinnamon

Pinch ground cloves

Pinch ground nutmeg

1 cup (240 ml) high-quality extra-virgin olive oil

1 cup (200 g) packed light brown sugar

2 large eggs

1 tablespoon (6 g) lemon zest

1½ cups (360 ml) water, for the cooking pot

3 tablespoons (23 g) confectioners' sugar, for dusting

💙 TOG TIPS!

Properly weighing and measuring the flour is very important; otherwise, you could end up with a paperweight.

If using a 6-cup (1.4 L) Bundt pan, halve the recipe and cook for 35 minutes.

1. Line the bottom and sides of a 7½- to 8-inch-round (19 to 20 cm) cake pan with parchment paper (see TOG Tips!). Set aside.

2. In a medium bowl, combine the apples, raisins, and orange juice. Soak for 30 minutes.

3. In another medium bowl, whisk together the flour, baking powder, baking soda, cinnamon, cloves, and nutmeg. Set aside.

4. In a large bowl, using a handheld electric mixer, beat together the olive oil and brown sugar until well combined. Add the eggs and beat for 1 minute.

5. Fold the flour mixture into the olive oil mixture with a wooden spoon and mix until fully incorporated. The batter will be very thick, but don't be tempted to add any more liquid.

6. Drain the orange juice from the raisins and apples. Fold the raisins and apples into the batter, along with the lemon zest, and mix until well combined. Pour the batter into the prepared pan and flatten it out with a spoon.

7. Place a stainless-steel trivet in the bottom of the cooking pot and add the water to the pot. Using a foil sling, lower the cake pan onto the trivet.

8. Lock the lid and close the pressure valve. Cook for 50 minutes on High Pressure for an 8-inch (20 cm) pan and 55 minutes on High Pressure for a 7½-inch (19 cm) pan. When the beep sounds, wait 10 minutes, then release the remaining pressure.

9. Remove the lid, then remove the cake from the pressure cooker. Cool completely.

10. Remove the cake from the pan and dust with confectioners' sugar right before serving.

Index

ACKNOWLEDGMENTS

To my dad, Leonard Selkowitz. You gave me my brains, ethics, kindness, cooking skills, compassion, and, unfortunately, a weight issue. You are the best person I have ever known. I love you so much more than I ever told you and I always felt your love. You were my cheerleader, my teacher, and always so proud of me, no matter what I did—well, except singing. When you told me that I couldn't carry a tune, I knew I must be pretty bad. I miss you so much and wish you could have seen me finally doing what I truly love.

To Chester and Junie Moon. You both are my heart. Your unconditional love and purrs make even a bad day wonderful. Your personal supervision by sitting on my desk, blocking my computer screen, standing on my keyboard, and sitting on my lap has kept me in check. During the writing of this book, I lost my kitties, Katie, Chester, and Jacob. I miss you all every day, especially, Chester, who never left my side for almost twenty years.

To Edward Martino. The man who continues to take my breath away. I want to give you extra special thanks for your support of me and my dreams. The little ways you show your love for me do not go unnoticed. I want you to know how much you are appreciated, not just because you clean up my messes—sometimes twice a day—but because you do so with a kind heart and without complaint. We have traveled a long piece of road together, and I look forward to each day with you on this daily adventure we call life.

To my sounding boards and sanity keepers: Kathy Betit Gallagher, Karla Maez and Heather Falkinburg Zima. You were there for me during the early days, and I know that you are part of why I am where I am now, doing what I love, sharing it, and building a kind community.

To my readers, community members, and other wonderful humans I've met along the way. For without you, this book would not be possible. You encourage me every day. You put a smile on my face every day. You are the ones who support and inspire me and have allowed me to fulfill my dreams. From the bottom of my heart, I thank you lovely and beautiful people. Many of you express your gratitude for my help and support, and I can only hope that you already know that the benefits go both ways. The relationships between us are vital to how it all works. Thank you for your longstanding support and participation!

To Lisa MarcAurele and Naan Gemdilio. Thank you for your patience and the miracle of your understanding. You really "get" me, and that is a wonderful thing. Your friendship, honesty, advice, and support mean the world to me.

P.S. Do you smell the aroma of onions and garlic?